D1288931

PAT SMYTHE'S BOOK OF HORSES

Prince Hal winning the Gioucestershire Area International Trial at Badminton

PAT SMYTHE'S BOOK OF HORSES

CASSELL & COMPANY LTD
LONDON

CASSELL & COMPANY LTD
35 Red Lion Square · London WC1
and at
MELBOURNE · SYDNEY · TORONTO · CAPE TOWN
· JOHANNESBURG · AUCKLAND

First Edition, October 1955
Second Edition, January 1956
Third Edition, September 1956
Fourth Edition, January 1957
Fifth Edition, October 1957
Sixth Edition, October 1958
Seventh Edition, November 1959

Reprinted by Lithography in Great Britain by
Jarrold & Sons Ltd, Norwich
859

Preface

THIS is the mechanical age, as people soon realize when they try to cross London on a weekday, or travel at Bank Holidays. The machine, however, will never oust the horse, and in some places a motor will never be able to replace the work done by horses. While I was in Texas, I was lucky enough to help in the cattle round-up on a huge ranch. It was both a joy and an education to see the cattle-ponies, tough and sure footed, wheeling and turning, and pulling up dead from a gallop as they cut out the cattle. Again, with Tschiffely's famous ride from Buenos Aires to Washington, which is described in a chapter in this book, Mancha and Gato, his sturdy Criollo ponies, carried him safely over mountain ranges and through jungles where even the toughest car could never have penetrated.

Whether used for work or pleasure, a horse can be an absorbing study and a wonderful friend. Horses are in some ways rather like children, but they will always remember good or bad treatment, and know whom they can trust. They respond well to affectionate firmness, but they do not respect weak sentimentality, or give of their best to a rider who tries to beat them into subjection. If you are lucky enough to own a pony, learn to understand his character, and treat him well. There is almost no greater pleasure than to earn the love and loyalty of 'that wonderful, one-two-three-four-legged friend' of the cowboy song.

It would take several books much longer than this to cover the whole story of horses. I have tried to pick out different aspects that I hope will interest the reader. It will be reward enough if my book encourages a few more boys and girls to discover the fun and value of riding.

Pat Smythe

Acknowledgements

GRATEFUL acknowledgement is due to the following sources for their permission to reproduce the photographs used in this book. The numbers indicate the pages on which the photographs appear.

L'Année Hippique, Lausanne: 18, 32, 33, 56(2), 57, 58(2), 64; Barratt's Photo Press: 63; British Horse Society: 35, 42, 53, 60, 61, 62; Camera Press Ltd.: 86, 88, 89, 90, 91, 92, 93, 95; J. Allan Cash: 38; The Commissioner of Police: 99, 100; The Greyhound Racing Association: 24, 29; P. A. Harding: Frontispiece; Harringay Arena Ltd: 54, 59; *Irish Times*: 28, 30; Kemsley Picture Service: 17, 19, 29, 66, 68, 69, 72; A. E. Lamorisse, Paris: 7, 120; Roger Lyon, Paris: 64; Miles Brothers: 1, 2(2), 4, 5, 8, 13(3), 14(3), 15, 75, 76, 77, 78, 81, 98, 103; Mirrorpic: 70, 73; P.A.-Reuter: 27; Picture Post Library: 26, 67, 71; The Pony Club: 9, 10; Sport and General: 12, 20, 21, 22, 25, 31, 48, 49, 50, 51, 97; Topical Press Agency: 40, 83; Mrs. Tschiffely: 105, 106, 108, 109, 111, 113; United States Information Service: 6.

Contents

Arab Stallion

Chapter One

HORSES

ALTHOUGH the ancestry and heredity of the horses of the British Isles is complex, it is fair to say that they are descended from three main roots: the native mountain and moorland ponies, which developed from the prehistoric horse whose pictures and remains were found in the caves of Spain and Southern France; the 'great horse' of the Middle Ages, whose ancestors were probably the horses of the Fens and Midlands; and the Arabian horse. Many famous specimens of the Arabian horse were imported into England at the end of the seventeenth and beginning of the eighteenth centuries. The 'great horse' was the result of the military methods of the Middle Ages, when riders were heavily armoured knights and men-at-arms. With this weight, plus the armour carried by the horse itself, it is easy to understand why these horses had to be so big and strong.

With the arrival of gunpowder, the heavy horse would probably have died out altogether had it not been for the development of wheeled transport and the need for a strong horse able to pull laden farm carts through clay and mud. It is, then, from the eighteenth century that our heavy breeds date—Shire, Suffolk, and Clydesdale, with the later importation of the French Percheron.

There is no doubt, however, that the supreme achievement in horse-breeding is the production of the English Thoroughbred. The original strain was developed in the time of King Charles II, and the Thoroughbred is now acknowledged to be the most beautiful specimen of the whole equine race. There are two main reasons for this: the special qualities of the British soil and climate, and the Arabian ancestors.

Lester Piggot on Never Say Die,
winner of the 1954 Derby

The most typical of all British horses today is probably the heavyweight hunter. Brave, bold, and intelligent, having good manners and a quietness of temperament, with solid bone and good broad feet—those are the qualities which enable a hunter to carry himself and his rider for many miles on a day's hunting across heavy plough and pasture land.

Patience must be one of its greatest virtues. Without becoming over-excited it must be prepared to stand outside a covert waiting for hounds to find. At the same time it must be alert and ready to gallop off when the right moment comes. On returning to the stables it must be calm, so that it does not break out in a sweat during the night or fuss and worry about its day with hounds. We used to have trouble with Tosca who would think about

Champion Hunter

her hunting all night, sweating and losing condition instead of relaxing and eating her supper.

In the show ring, the hunter classes are usually divided into three sections: the heavy-weight, who must be able to carry the weight of rider and saddle from 14 st. 7 lb. and upwards; the middleweight, for weights of between 14 st. 7 lb. and 13 st.; and the light-weight, which is restricted to under 13 st.

It is useful to know what the judges are looking for in the show ring. A good hunter must have presence, with a good head straight-fronted and well-proportioned and not heavy-looking or coarse. A heavy head or weak neck produces a tired horse very quickly. The eyes are important. They should be large and kind, well set apart with wide and clear vision. As an indication of character and blood, the ears should be small and clean, always in motion, pricking forward or turning back. It is in its ears that the horse's emotions and changes of mood are reflected.

Its body should be well made and solid, well coupled with short and muscled loins and powerful hindquarters. The chest should be wide and deep to give plenty of room for heart and lungs, so that it can gallop far and fast. The quarters, from which comes its propelling power, must be strong and well-developed, with long solid muscles. The feet should be well-shaped and big enough for the animal's height, weight, and size. As opposed to a race-horse, which for speed must have smaller and lighter feet, a heavyweight hunter needs bigger and tougher hooves.

The hack is a lighter type of horse than the hunter, although its manners must be no less perfect and its patience equally sound. The name 'hack', which is essentially British and of quite ancient origin, must not be confused with the name 'hackney' which is the name given to the show breed of harness-horse.

The hack, which is not an established breed, is any horse or pony which is suitable for riding, although certain standards are laid down by the British Show Hack and Cob Association. These state that the animal must not exceed 15·3 hands but can be of any colour.

To win in the show ring, any horse which conforms to this height and possesses the necessary quality and manners may be of any breed, but in practice it is natural that the winner is usually the Thoroughbred, for quality and presence are the guiding factors. There-fore, all the best points that one expects to find in an attractive Thoroughbred are needed also in the winning hack. Its manners must be

Mrs. Cook on Alexander, a winning Cob

infallible. It must be trained to stand perfectly still while the rider mounts and dismounts, and to walk with ease and freedom, using its shoulders and turning its head neither to right nor left. Similarly with the trot, it must be capable of collection or extension as asked by the rider. This also applies to the canter when it must move smoothly, showing no knee-action. In addition, it must be able to perform such movements as a figure-of-eight, with a change of leg, turn on the forehand or haunches, a half pass to either side, and reining back.

A high-class hack must always give the impression of being under perfect control, willing to obey the rider's instructions without effort or hesitation. It should give a display of extreme balance and beauty of action, controlled and elegant.

The hackney, on the other hand, with its characteristic high-stepping trotting action, is today used only in the show classes. It is purely a harness-horse. Its origins go a long way back into English history, for the trotting horse was mentioned in 1303. The name itself comes from the Norman-French word, *haquenée*.

However, the immediate ancestor of the modern hackney is the Norfolk Trotter, which sprang from the blood of two horses, an Arab stallion and a Yorkshire stallion in about 1729. The Norfolk Roadster, as it was called, was a heavily built, powerful animal used by farmers. It was fast and had great stamina, and very often had to carry not only the farmer to market but his wife also, riding pillion behind him. The most famous of that breed was the Norfolk Cob, said to have trotted 24 miles in the hour, and definitely on record as having done 2 miles in 5 minutes 4 seconds. During the nineteenth century, with the arrival of the railway, the Norfolk breed lost favour, but was revived again by the Hackney Horse Society as the animal we see today.

In addition to its fiery paces, its chief characteristics are: small convex head and small muzzle; small ears and large eyes; long, thick-set head; powerful shoulders and low withers. A compact body is important. The tail used to be docked, set and carried high, but there is a rule now that prevents the docking of horses. A lengthy foreleg gives good action and the hind legs need strong hocks well let down. Its feet are well shaped and it has a fine silky coat. The most popular colours are dark brown, black, bay, and chestnut.

Mrs. Haydon driving the champion Hackney Hurstwood Superlative

There can be no mistaking the hackney, particularly when it is moving. The free shoulder action and high knee action, with the foreleg thrown well forward and a slight pause of the foot at each stride, gives it an unusual grace of movement. The present-day hackney has far more quality than was necessary thirty years ago—when the breed needed the substance for road work. Since the advent of the internal-combustion engine, which threw the horse off the road, the hackney has to provide an elegant exhibition to delight the public all over the world.

One of our most popular horses is the Riding Cob, which is not in itself a breed but a type, with a personality and character of its own. Although it is smaller than the hunter and often much heavier, it is by no means useless in the hunting field, and what it lacks in speed it makes up in sense and intelligence. Primarily, however, it is intended for use as a heavyweight hack for the more elderly rider, and its excellent manners and smaller size make it ideal for employment in this way.

It is impossible to fix exactly the origin of the cob, though its foundation might well be

Team of Grey Shire Geldings

similar to the Welsh Cob's. There is no doubt, however, that many successful show-ring cobs are closely related to half-bred cart mares and heavyweight hunter mares put to stallions of quality.

The greatest of England's agricultural horses, the Shire Horse, is one of the most respected of all our breeds. It is bred mainly in the heavy-soiled counties of Lincoln, Huntingdon, and Cambridge. With its enormous strength, and standing over 17 hands, it is able to pull a weight of 5 tons. Steady and docile, at three years old it can be worked on farms and very quickly becomes a commercial proposition. Many breweries have magnificent teams of Shires, which can be seen at some of the agricultural shows throughout the country.

The Shire's origin can be traced to the breed of heavy horse in existence in Elizabethan times, the 'great horse' of England mentioned at the beginning of this chapter. It came to be known by its present name, Shire Horse, some two hundred years ago.

Famous throughout the world, and the best known of all British breeds, is the Thoroughbred. So proud are we of its fame and achievements that sometimes we tend to forget that it has foreign blood, and is only called 'English' because it has been bred and developed here for so long. In fact, 'thoroughbred' is the literal translation of the Arabic *kehilan*, meaning pure-bred all through.

All Thoroughbreds trace their ancestry to three well-known Arabian shires—the Darley Arabian, the Godolphin Arabian, and the Byerley Turk. It has often been suggested that these famous horses were put to English mares, but there can be no doubt that the foundation mares were Eastern mares, probably Arabian. In time, less Arab blood was introduced and the quest for speed became all-important. Now, the Thoroughbred can beat the Arab in any speed test and has, in fact, become a racing machine. It has a name synonymous with the race-horse or, more personally, with Prince Hal whom I bought after seeing him racing at Cheltenham.

Galcador, winner of the 1950 Derby

The value of the breed is, therefore, based almost entirely on speed and those which cannot win races, or breed foals, tend to become valueless. Smaller Thoroughbreds with the necessary substance and balance may make excellent polo ponies.

Together with the Arab, the Thoroughbred is the most beautiful horse in the world, with its refined head, arched and elegant neck, pronounced wither, and sloping shoulder. Its whole appearance gives the impression of great quality and intense speed.

People interested in horse-breeding know about America's 'Blue Grass Country' in Kentucky, where the country's great breeding establishments are situated. It is the home of American race-horses and trotting horses. The great advantage of this fertile land is its rainfall which occurs evenly throughout the year. Actually, when I was there in the autumn of 1953, there had been a bad drought, and instead of rolling green pastures, the fields were brown and burnt up, with the stock having to be fed on hay. The soil contains sufficient natural phosphate for the growth of grass at its very best, and it is claimed that the best land around Lexington, the centre of Kentucky, has from six to ten times as much phosphate as the best corn-growing soils in the United States. So, like parts of Ireland, the 'Blue Grass Country' is the ideal nursery for the horse.

Nevertheless, horses are bred in many parts of the United States, especially where they are needed for cattle work, such as on the ranches in Texas. It is the same in South America, where at once we think of the Criollo, the polo pony, and the cow pony, those tough and untiring workers.

One example of the extraordinary powers of endurance of the Criollo is illustrated by the two famous horses, Mancha and Gato, which carried Professor A. F. Tschiffely from Buenos Aires to New York. At the ages of sixteen and eighteen they covered 13,350 miles at an average of 26·5 miles each day, achieving a record in altitude of 19,250 feet. They also travelled 93 miles across a desert in Ecuador without water in a temperature of 120 degrees. It was an amazing journey and probably only horses of the Criollo's strength and stamina could ever have made it.

It is generally believed that Christopher Columbus was responsible for introducing the horse into America, although it is certain that the early settlers in the North American continent found it necessary to introduce horses, and did in fact import them.

Farther north, in Canada, although it covers such a vast area, the country has never been well known for its horse-breeding. It is true that horses are bred there but it is not regarded as a national industry.

Canada is known for its severe winters and great extremes of temperature which are a distinct disadvantage. It is for this reason, as much as any, that Canada is unable to claim any particular breed of horse as her own.

One of the breeds in which America takes great pride is the Saddle Horse. Its speciality is the gaits which it exhibits in the show ring. The animals are specially trained in each gait and are known as either three- or five-gaited horses according to this training. These gaits are the usual walk, trot, and canter, together with the artificial paces, the running walk, stepping pace or slow rack, and fast rack. Therefore, a three-gaited horse is capable of carrying out the first three movements, while a five-gaited horse can do the specialized gaits as well.

The trot must be highly collected, with the head well flexed, neck and tail arched. The action must be high, smooth, and speedy. The rack is a single-footed pace, each foot coming down singly and very fast with no pauses. At an order from the judge of 'Rack on!' it is increased into a stepping pace, very fast with the feet on each side following each other instead of stepping diagonally as in the ordinary trot. They cover the ground at a great rate, with the rider bumping up and down and not attempting to rise as for the trot. When the O.K. is given for 'racking on' there is great excitement in the show ring. The horses speed up, racing round the ring, passing each other, while the riders sit back and encourage their horses to catch the judge's eye. The dock of the horse's tail is broken to give it that rather false, set look, and very high carriage, and the whole performance provides quite a different spectacle from our show classes in England.

The breed comes from the early pioneering days over 400 years ago, when there were only two ways of moving about the vast stretches of the new continent, on water or on horseback. There was no native horse in America at that time, so the early settlers brought their own or imported them later on. English amblers and pacers were introduced before the days of the Thoroughbred, together with horses from Spain, Africa, France, and the East. All these contributed towards the American Saddle Horse.

Morgan Saddle Horse

The pioneers had to have a strong, light horse, fast and comfortable to ride over long distances, adaptable to harness, intelligent, and

The *gardiens* rounding up the white horses of the Camargue

good-tempered. They therefore bred with care from the best stock available, eventually including the English Thoroughbred, and this gave the breed its fire and brilliance. Over a period, other American strains have been introduced.

Another interesting American breed is the Tennessee or Plantation Walking Horse. Its name indicates the special reason for which it was introduced, to carry the planters and farmers at a comfortable pace over their plantations. It can be ridden at a fast running walk, and yet move so smoothly that a rider, not rising in the saddle, can carry a full glass of water without spilling a drop. It is a heavier and more powerful animal than the American Saddle Horse, and is usually stouter, more robust, and altogether less elegant. It carries its head very high and has great knee action for the running walk, but it can also be ridden at the ordinary walk, and canter, and is a good trotter in harness. This breed is also used for agricultural work on farms. They are first-class general purpose animals whether it be on the farm, between the shafts, or under saddle.

The Palomino, from California, lives up to its name of 'the golden horse of the West'. Its colour is literally gold and has been compared to a United States gold coin. Except for a very light, almost white mane and tail, and for white on the face and legs, the pure Palomino has no other colours or markings. Palominos are very popular with the cowboys who use them as parade horses, and they look wonderful when covered by embroidered trappings and the western saddlery worked with Mexican silver and leather trimmings.

Horses of this colour were at one time highly prized in Spain, where Queen Isabella, the sponsor of Columbus, encouraged their breeding. It is possible that Columbus took some Palominos to the West Indies. Cortez had them in Mexico in 1519 and it was there that he presented one to Jean de Palomino, from whom they get their name.

However, they were not rediscovered until over a hundred years ago, when the United States took possession of California in 1848 after the Mexican War. At that time, the Palomino was used only as a saddle-horse, and for parades and other displays. Its popularity declined until recently, when its striking appearance and excellent riding qualities became fully appreciated.

The American Quarter Horse, used by cowboys for cattle work, has an interesting origin. In the early days in Virginia, the first horse racing in America was carried out along short improvised tracks, since there were insufficient cleared sites to lay down proper racecourses. These tracks were normally about a quarter of a mile long, so the horse which was bred to race on them was called the 'Quarter Horse'. Naturally, for this kind of racing, a very quick starter and fast sprinter was required and, amongst others, it is these qualities which the cowboys find so useful. For their purpose, their horses must also be capable of stopping and turning out of a flat-out gallop. They must be well balanced and quick on their feet when it is necessary to catch a cow or calf that is trying to dodge back into the herd. In addition, their great strength gives them the power to hold a heavy steer when it is roped. I was given one of these horses to ride when helping the cowboys to cut out cattle. I was most impressed by its calmness of temperament and superb balance in spite of the quick starts and changes of speed. The horse knew how to work cattle and taught me a great deal.

It is impossible to mention every breed or type of horse within the limits of one chapter. Every country has developed its own type to suit its particular climate and conditions. In Australia, the famous breed of the Waler is the stand-by of Australian cattle men. These robust horses were bred in New South Wales for the Indian Army during the nineteenth century and have since proved good all-rounders, even jumping record heights in the show ring.

From the Far East, we adorn our mantelpieces with those attractive little china horses, showing their antics when stung by a bee.

Our own pony breeds are unique throughout the world, and in no other country have children such a good opportunity of getting their initial experience on mounts that are the right size. One of the charms of the countryside is to see these mountain and moorland ponies in their natural surroundings. When they are broken in they make the most ideal companions and friends for the children who own them.

There are many volumes in our libraries written about the breeds of horses that have played such an important part throughout the ages. All these writings bear testimony to the value of one of the best loved of our domestic animals, which has now for so long served man for his pleasure and his daily needs.

Chapter Two

THE PONY CLUB

THE Pony Club has grown unbelievably since it was founded in 1929 and now has become a world-wide institution with branches in the Commonwealth and America. There are 203 branches in Great Britain and Northern Ireland, and 148 affiliated branches overseas. Usually they are linked territorially with the various hunts, and by means of rallies, lectures, camps, and competitions, young riders have the best opportunities of getting first-class instruction in horsemanship at little cost. The chief object of the Club is to encourage young people to ride and to learn to enjoy all kinds of sport connected with horses and riding.

My Pony Club days during the last war gave me a great deal of fun, particularly as it was a chance to meet other children when horses or bicycles were the only method of transport. We used to organize Mock Hunts, and I usually got the job of 'fox', probably because I knew the country and the best places for jumping. These Mock Hunts were invaluable training for the time when we could take our places in the hunting field, because they were run on exactly the same lines as a proper hunt.

The best riders used to act as hounds, with one of the senior members as Field Master whose job was to control the field, which was made up by the rest of the riders. My job as fox was to lay the trail with powdered whitewash. We never used paper because for one thing there was not much to spare during the war, and, more important, because it makes such a litter all over the countryside. Also, it can very easily blow away from the trail and in wet weather it gets soggy and is very hard to see.

The fox was given an hour's start and, with a lump of whitewash in my mackintosh pocket, I galloped off to lay the trail by putting white dabs of 'scent' on stones or walls and trees, and

A Pony Club meet in Canada

Cleaning tack in a Pony Club camp in Australia

to set clues. Sometimes when it rained the whitewash would consolidate in my pocket and the result would be disastrous for the mackintosh. The clues were always kept in small glass tubes so that they could not get wet, and were hidden away in various places, such as the branches of a tree, at a height at which they could be untied without dismounting. It was entirely up to the hounds to find them, as also the whitewash marks showing the trail, and although the field read the clues they were never allowed to look at them until hounds had marked them by giving tongue—though some of the enthusiastic 'music' was quite unique, and would certainly have baffled proper hounds!

Sometimes I would lay a false trail with a clue at the end of it reading: 'You're on a fresh fox. Make a cast.' Then the Master had to make a proper cast until hounds found the right trail again. If the Master made a quick and accurate cast, while the fox was getting involved in laying the fresh trail, hounds had a very good chance of catching him before he reached his earth, and the lemonade and buns waiting for him! Every tradition of the hunting field was strictly observed during these Mock Hunts, and not only did we get an immense amount of fun out of them but we were constantly learning things which would be of use to us later on.

Up to the age of twenty-one anyone, boy or girl, can join the Pony Club by paying the prescribed entrance fee and annual subscription. Those who are lucky enough to have a farmer father, and have hounds hunting over his land, will be exempted from paying the entrance fee. The affairs of the Club are managed by the Pony Club Organization Committee, which is controlled and directed by the British Horse Society in London. For the purpose of forming branches, Great Britain and Northern Ireland is divided into districts which correspond, as nearly as possible, to the Hunts, and the branches are named after the Hunts in whose district they are situated. They are controlled locally by their own Local Committee under the direction of a District Commissioner. The rules permit any member to transfer to another branch, although no one is allowed to belong to two branches at the same time, except as an honorary member. Membership badges can be bought at a small charge and have to be worn at branch rallies, when hunting, and at shows.

These rallies are one of the main features of Club activities. Interesting instruction is nearly always given, followed by games and sports where the schooling that has been taught can be put into practice. There is a preference for team work as opposed to individual competition so that nobody need feel that they are left out. We used to have great games of 'French and English' over the ancient battlefield of Lansdown near Bath. The opposing sides would have their lines each side of no-man's-land. The smaller ponies had a great advantage in being able to sneak round into the enemy lines, unnoticed behind the bushes and bumps. The faster ponies were always useful for rescuing the prisoners, but there was a job for everyone and one soon learnt that complete control was necessary over the ponies if Red Indian tactics were to be successfully adopted.

Dismounted rallies are also held, when visits to kennels and riding establishments, and lectures, and other events are arranged. Unlike the continual struggle to find the winner in show classes, there are no awards at the working rallies but there might be prizes at those organized for competitive sport, such as gymkhanas, hunter trials, or combined training. The prizes normally consist of rosettes. The riders compete for the honour of winning and not for financial gain, so money awards are never given. Sometimes prizes in kind, such as a hoof pick or a Dandy brush, might be presented by a kind parent in addition to rosettes, and I remember once winning a very useful Red Cross outfit to carry on my saddle when riding. For the first time I was proudly able to use the rings on the saddle to fix the bag. My pony was not too keen on the extra attachment tickling its side but, after an indignant rodeo display when it found that the thing didn't budge, it soon took no notice. In fact, after that I was able to tie on to the saddle the odd rabbits caught by the dogs, instead of putting them down the front of my wind jacket, which didn't improve the state of my clothes!

To encourage Club members to improve their knowledge, and to stimulate interest in the standard of their work, there are a series of tests which members can take, and for each of these an Efficiency Certificate is awarded. There are four in all—A, B, C, and D—with A the highest and D the lowest. D is quite an easy one to pass, the main requirements being keenness and an ability just to ride, bridle, and saddle a pony, and to mount and dismount correctly. The others are progressively more difficult, and to gain the Efficiency Certificate for Standard A the member's knowledge and proficiency have to be very sound. As each test is passed, a different coloured ribbon can be worn on the Pony Club Badge.

There is always great interest in the official Pony Club Inter-Branch Competition, which consists of a number of Area Competitions followed by the final Championships. The three phases of dressage, cross-country, and show jumping are held on one day, but on the same lines as a Three-Day Event. This has already helped to encourage a high standard of riding throughout the Club and many ex-Pony Club riders are ready to train for international events. Interest in riding as a sport and recreation has been stimulated in this way amongst the younger generation.

One of the most popular events among the children is the Summer Camp, when members spend a week under canvas, or sometimes in a farmhouse or barn. Not only is it a wonderful holiday, but it gives the chance to put into practice all the things that have been learnt in theory. Concentrated work of every description is carried out, with special instruction, gymkhanas, lectures, and plenty of riding.

Two Pony Club members try to stake the first claim to the last pole in a gymkhana event

Interesting people come down to visit the camps and perhaps give demonstrations or show films. The riders and their ponies can really get fit and progress with riding every day. The difficulty of occasional rides is that both ponies and riders can forget a little of the things they have already learnt, then by the time they are back in their stride they are too tired to learn any more. Riding, like any sport, uses certain muscles that normally are not exercised. Likewise with the ponies, when they are brought up off grass after a lazy time in the field during the term, they are naturally short of wind until they have had some work to get them fit. There is nothing more disheartening or tiring than having constantly to kick the fat sides of a pony in an effort to keep up with the other riders. However, if the pony is rationed, and has a reasonable figure by the beginning of the holidays, a child will not get nearly so tired or stiff at first. After a few days of ordinary hacking, they will be ready for anything.

When children are riding a pony, I wonder if they ever think of his origin, of the great long line of ancestors which stretches out behind him to far away prehistoric days. It is very easy to take him for granted and never think about where he first came from or how he was bred. Actually, nobody has ever been able to decide definitely about the origin of the native ponies of the British Isles, except that this does go back to prehistoric times. So they have always been described by the names of the nine locations in which they have been found from time immemorial: Connemara, Dartmoor, Exmoor, the Dales and Fells of Durham, Northumberland, and Cumberland, the New Forest, the Highlands, the Shetland Islands, and the Welsh Mountains. There is a tenth area—Lundy Island—which is also the home of a type of semi-wild pony.

All these ponies have many points in common: smallness of size and yet great strength in relation to it; a stocky build; toughness and endurance; adaptability and high intelligence. Most of them have always been used as children's ponies, but even more often as the foundation stock, by mating with Arab or Thoroughbred, for the type of children's pony seen in the show ring. They are extremely beautiful animals ranging from 12 hands to 14·2 hands, with the small hunter up to 15·2 hands.

Individual details of the different breeds naturally vary quite considerably.

Connemara

Dartmoor Pony

Connemara: This is the district in Connaught, north of Galway Bay and west of Loughs Corrib and Mask. The breed is of very ancient origin and believed to be associated more recently with Spanish and Barb blood, some say from the animals which survived the wreck of the Spanish Armada off the west coast of Ireland in 1588. Not until 1928 were any serious attempts made to preserve and improve the breed. These ponies reach up to 14 hands, or more, in height, and have a very kindly temperament with great jumping ability. Their predominant colour is grey.

Dartmoor: This breed has practically disappeared from its native home, the pure blood having deteriorated by the admixture of Shetland strains. Some private breeders have preserved pure-bred ponies, but they are used more often as foundation stock than children's ponies. Their height seldom exceeds 12·2 hands, and they are mostly brown, black, or bay in colour. Pixie, my first pony, was a Dartmoor crossed with an Arab and bred on the Prince of Wales' Farm by Tor Royal on Dartmoor. She had the Prince of Wales' feathers branded on her near shoulder. The inclusion of Arab blood probably accounted for her size of 13·1 hands and chestnut colour with four white socks.

Exmoor Stallion

Exmoor: This breed from Somerset almost certainly had the same ancestry as their close neighbours from Dartmoor, although they have not yet suffered the same deterioration. They are about the same size, but are grey in colour as well as brown and bay. A mealy-coloured nose is usually one of their characteristics.

Dales: These ponies are from the Upper Dales of Tyne, Allen, Tees, and Wear. In historic times they were used as pack ponies to carry lead ore from the mines of Durham and Northumberland to the sea. Today they are bred for harness. Like miniature cart-horses to look at, they are sturdy and strong, and have feathered heels. Their main colours are black, brown, and bay.

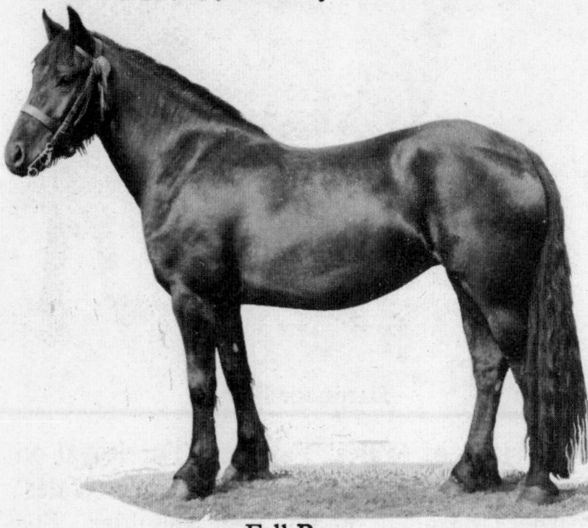

Fell Pony

Fell: Like the Dales, these ponies from the fells of Westmorland and Cumberland were once pack ponies carrying lead ore from the Pennines to the North Sea ports. Smaller than the Dales, they are more pony-like and, though docile, are extremely strong and unsuitable for small children. Their predominant colour is black. Bay rarely receives consideration in a show class.

New Forest Pony

New Forest: Another ancient breed, although its accessibility has been responsible for many foreign strains. They are the most popular and suitable native breeds for children, being not so wide and stocky as the ordinary moorland ponies although a little taller, and often running to 14 hands. Favourite colours are bay and brown. We have found that they have excellent temperaments for children. If one buys them unbroken at the fairs, they are easier to break in than the wilder Welsh ponies, probably because they have more contact with humans in the New Forest.

Shetland: This is the smallest of the breeds because of the scanty forage and very hard life of the windswept northern islands where it lives. They are proud of their smallness and are officially measured in inches, not hands. Forty-two inches is considered to be the absolute maximum, and any Shetland pony higher than this is not considered particularly valuable. The average is about 39 inches. In appearance, it looks like a miniature heavy horse on deer's legs. It has a determined temperament and great intelligence.

Welsh Stallion

Welsh: From the Welsh border and central Wales. This breed is the acknowledged aristocrat of all the native breeds, its great beauty probably owing much to Arab blood, which is evident in its whole appearance and particularly in the tail and head carriage. There are three sections to this breed: Welsh mountain pony, Welsh cob pony, and Welsh cob.

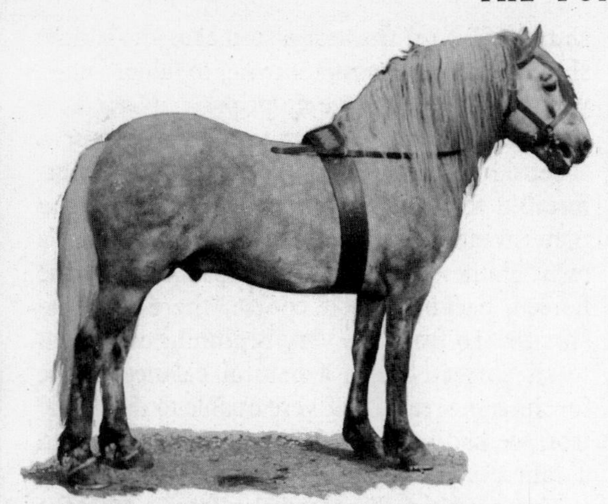

Mr. Lamont's Highland Pony, winner of class for Highland Stallions

Highland: This breed is found in the Western Highlands and the Western Isles. The smallest—12·2 to 13·2 hands—comes from Barra, the larger—up to 14·2 hands—from the mainland. An all-purpose breed, they are useful in agriculture for pack and draught, and are tireless when carrying heavy weights. They are used by the highlanders for bringing down off the mountains deer shot by the stalkers during the season. The most popular colours are black, brown, dun, and grey.

Lundy: Lundy Island is off the North Devon coast. This is a distinctive breed though not officially recognized. It is of mixed blood, deriving from certain selected sires, including a Galloway—a Scottish breed now extinct—and New Forest mares. The ponies live wild and do not grow heavy coats in the winter. They are well known for their natural jumping abilities and have extremely good feet. Their average height is 13 hands.

The *polo pony* is a type rather than a breed, and as long as the game of polo has existed so has the polo pony. And the game has been going for a very long time, having been played in the Far East, from Persia to Japan, for at least 2,000 years. The only standard by which a polo pony is judged is its performance. Some of the best in the world would never have got a prize in any show class. The top-class ponies may be nothing to look at, but 'handsome is as handsome does'. They have to be able to gallop at full speed, stop in their own length, turn or swing round, and start again at top speed in any direction. All this with perhaps a very heavy rider. Therefore, the most important thing a polo pony should have is a light mouth. A judge would look for good shoulders, short strong back, and well-sprung ribs, powerful quarters, and strong hocks well let down. Together with sound conformation they need good balance, intelligence, and a courageous, honest temperament.

One of the many things which members of a Pony Club learn is elementary first aid. This knowledge is vital in caring for the pony at home and it is now necessary to know what to look for if, say, their pony goes lame during a ride. If it has any heat in its legs, the cause may be a blow, a strain, or a kick, and immediate treatment may save weeks of lameness. They should be able to wash out a cut—with Epsom-salts and water to draw out any dirt or infection—and give an anti-tetanus injection to guard against this disastrous germ.

In addition to first aid, members are taught how to look after their ponies. Grooming is most important and it is necessary always to make sure that the pony is comfortable, otherwise it will give a very uncomfortable ride and maybe put itself out of action for the holidays. One source of irritation to the animal could be a lump of mud under the saddle, or a badly fitting saddle which pinches, or perhaps the bridle is the wrong length, or a narrow bit rubbing its lips.

They are taught never to abuse the pony's mouth and to keep their hands light. If they do have to catch hold of something to keep their balance, the neck strap or mane is the best life line, never the reins. Their 'anchor' must never interfere with the pony's mouth, because if they do hold on by the reins as a security line it will never learn to respond properly to their movements and aids when they are riding.

They will be told how essential it is to clean the bit thoroughly when they come in from a ride, and that if any pieces of grass are left on it they will harden and rub the pony's mouth the next time they go out. Any sweat and mud should be wiped off the bridle with a wet cloth or, if it is very dirty, washed off and then saddle soap or glycerine soap applied to soften and preserve the leather.

I remember how careful we had to be, when the ponies had not been ridden at all during term time, to make sure that the girth did not rub a gall when we took them out for the first few times. This was very likely to happen just behind the elbow, and so for the first week we always applied surgical spirit to harden the skin, and if possible for a day or two before we rode them. Sometimes we would put a piece of sheepskin or rubber tube round the girth until the skin was hardened. We learnt by experience that prevention is better than cure, because a girth gall can take a very long time to heal and, if the pony had been laid up, our riding would have been seriously curtailed during the holidays.

It is very tempting to have a highly polished leather saddle, which gleams in the sun as one rides proudly into the show ring. But too much shiny polish on the seat also makes the saddle slippery and it is most annoying to fall off when you find that you have no grip.

At home we all learnt to ride with just a sheepskin and surcingle. This is more comfortable than riding bareback, because if the pony sweats one does not make a mess of one's own clothes. Also, the sheepskin pads the horse's backbone. Of course, there were no stirrups, so from the very beginning we learnt to sit correctly with a natural balance. Since for the same reason we were unable to rise to the trot, we had to make the pony go straight into a canter and so avoided that interim period, jarring trotting. We were also taught to make the ponies canter slowly and collectedly. I am quite sure that the sheepskin and surcingle is ideal equipment when one first learns to ride, and would thoroughly recommend it to anyone who is just beginning.

Above all things, remember the regular care of the pony's feet. If he suddenly goes lame, look to see if he has picked up a stone and it is pressing against the frog. Keep him well shod and shod regularly—and never forget what Mr. Jorrocks said: 'No foot—no 'oss!'

Chapter Three

THE GRANDSTAND VIEW

It is easy to be critical from the grandstand. From there I have found that I can ride a perfect round, whereas it is not always so simple to perform from the back of a horse. The more you know about any sport, the more enjoyment you get from watching it. This is equally true of show jumping, which has become so popular within the last few years with thousands of people rapidly becoming more interested in the activities of riders and horses. Of these thousands, the majority have probably never sat in a saddle, yet they appreciate and admire the courage and vitality they see displayed in the ring. But this spectacle can give more enjoyment if one knows a little more about the sport, not necessarily the rules and regulations, although they are simple enough to learn, but something also of the problems which face rider and horse whenever they enter the arena. Then as a spectator one can genuinely establish a link with the competitors, and come to understand a little of the thoughts in their minds as they confront the obstacles. Thus, even without ever having ridden a horse, one can obtain the greatest possible pleasure from the sport.

Every jump sets its own particular problem. From the viewpoint of the rider in the ring each one looks very different from the way it looks to the spectator up in the grandstand. Sometimes the rider hears the public give a sudden gasp of admiration as he clears a fence which never gave him a second's anxiety, while the really difficult obstacle successfully negotiated is unnoticed because it looks comparatively easy from the stands.

Jumping a fence in the show ring can be divided into three different phases. First, the approach; second, the jump itself; and third, the landing and strides which follow, themselves quickly becoming part of the approach to the next obstacle. A careful study of these three phases, and the manner in which rider and horse tackle them together, is well worth while if you are really intent on discovering the sort of thing the competitor is up against.

The approach is the most important and there are many different schools of thought on the issues involved. Some believe that it can be left entirely to the horse on the grounds that, since it is able to arrange its strides successfully without a rider on its back, it can do so just as well with one. There are others who maintain that a slow, controlled approach is

Tosca jumping at the White City

necessary, with the rider himself guiding each stride to make sure the horse arrives at the jump in an accurate position to negotiate it.

I think the answer lies somewhere between the two. Although the first might be suitable for speed events over small obstacles, it has been proved to be impractical for the consistent jumping of large fences. The second does not allow for the pace and momentum required for a horse to jump with the minimum effort; apart from the fact that one hasn't a moment to lose when jumping against the clock. There is no doubt that the rider can help the horse to jump, by ensuring that it arrives at the best place for the take-off and is correctly balanced. However, if the rider always demands complete obedience, and then makes a drastic mistake himself, the horse has no chance to put itself right.

Therefore, for a successful jump both the horse and rider must be balanced, and must ensure that they have sufficient pace to give the impulsion necessary for the particular type of fence. The horse must be obedient so that the rider can control the length of stride. The whole movement is designed to bring the horse smoothly to the easiest point for it to take off and clear the obstacle.

The rider's main concern with the second phase, the jump itself, is one of hand movement and weight distribution. His weight must be placed so as to give the horse freedom of movement. His legs must be in the right position to keep balance and impulsion, and his hands light and sensitive, maintaining an even feeling with the horse's mouth. The whole effect should be one of easy co-operation, with no exaggerated style. Any unnecessary movement can only divert the horse's attention and efficiency.

The landing and the beginning of the approach to the next fence are an important part of the jump. As the horse's fore legs reach the ground, the rider keeps his weight forward so that the hind legs can clear the fence with ease. The moment the horse has landed, the

Miss Diana Mason in the Show Jumping phase of the Three-Day Event at Basle riding Tramella

Prince Hal jumping the first fence at the White City

rider must maintain his balance and be in control ready for the next fence. Having already decided on his plan for jumping the course in a speed class, he has started to turn the horse to left or right as its fore legs come to the ground, and therefore makes sure no time is wasted in the approach to the next obstacle. Much time can be saved if the horse is obedient enough to jump the fences at a slight angle if necessary. It is up to the rider to know how many risks he can take within reason.

The fences themselves vary quite considerably, whether at a country show or in an international arena. It is most important for the rider to 'walk the course' before each event. From the grandstand, it may often appear that the whole thing is carried out quite casually and at great speed, with the riders giving each jump no more than a superficial glance. Certainly one usually has to be fairly quick about it, since there is only a short time between events in which to study the course, but any appearance of casualness is entirely false. The competitor has already seen a plan of the layout of the course and his main concerns, when once he gets into the arena and begins to walk round, are the construction of the fences, the angles at which they are placed, and the distance between them. With experience he can assimilate all these points very quickly.

Prince Hal winning the Athlone Cup at the Royal Show in 1952

Some jumps are wide enough to let the rider choose the place where he goes over. This choice is governed entirely by the direction of approach, the line to the next jump, and, possibly, even the likes and dislikes of the particular horse he is riding. On the other hand, a narrow fence must be jumped in the middle. The purpose of the course designer is not to set an unnecessarily difficult problem, but to test the rider's judgment and the ability and obedience of the horse. Although the height of some obstacles may appear to present an impossible task, they are all built within the limits of fairness and designed to prove the horse's power of elevation. 'Spreads', such as triple bars, need to be jumped with more impulsion than the upright fences.

Nowadays when jumping a course the rider must be prepared for anything. The variety of obstacles is wide and each one presents a different test, so success can only be achieved by a precise, rhythmical approach varied in accordance with the demands of each fence. A good course will include spread and straight fences, at least one combination, and several changes of direction so that both rider and horse must be constantly on the alert for every moment of their round.

At one time there were no judging rules and show-jumping judges had to invent their own. Some of them awarded marks in accordance with the size of the jump, and, generally, as many marks were given for the water-jump as for all the others put together. This was not altogether surprising, since the water was often as much as 15 feet wide, and the fence in front quite probably 4 feet high. The only other type of 'spread' was a plain hurdle 6 feet in front of a gorsed hurdle. The first few jumps in the course were usually hurdles or brush fences, and could be marked on style or in any other way that happened to appeal to the judge. The gate, wall, and water-jumps followed. The gate and water were generally used for the jump-off, with the final jump-off over the gate. This was usually won with the gate at about 5 feet 4 inches.

The best hunting style was regarded by some judges as the criterion for awarding marks, but in the early days no marks were deducted for refusals. In fact, after three refusals the competitor would be asked to try the next jump. Even when Olympia started, competitors were allowed to circle before a fence, and far from being considered a waste of time the technique was looked upon as the correct thing to do. If you went fast, you lacked finesse.

Before the First World War, the courses at Olympia certainly bore some resemblance to those we have today, but the rounds were very slow and must have been very tiring to watch. There was no time limit and the judging organization was, by today's standards, most unwieldly. At each jump stood a judge with a book of slips, and with him a small boy in uniform. After marking his slip, the judge handed it to the boy and, when the competitor left the ring, the messenger ran as fast as he could to a collecting point on the rails. The confusion must have been considerable, with a number of small boys converging from all parts of the ring upon the chief judge, whose job it was to sort out the slips and add up the points. Even when I started jumping at small shows the course would always consist of a hurdle as the first fence, a sheep pen of hurdles to make an in-and-out for the second fence, followed by the traditional post and

Tosca receiving the Coronation Champion Challenge Cup at Richmond Royal Horse Show in 1952

Tosca

rails, gate, wall, and triple bar, and finishing with a flat-out gallop up the centre of the ring over the water-jump. It was not against the rules to walk or trot between fences and one usually pulled up to loosen the horse's martingale, in order to give it the necessary freedom to clear the water.

Today, with a continual growth in the popularity of show jumping, the organizers are always at great pains to consider the spectators and ensure that something of interest is always happening in the ring. This applies equally in the small show as it does in the international arena. No one wants to sit through a competition lasting three hours or more; both riders and spectators would be bored by the monotony long before the final arrived. The same applies to a jump-off, which most show-jumping spectators like to see. But they prefer it to be between a select few and not half the original number of competitors, as does sometimes happen at a badly organized show.

The aim of any show, large or small, must be to provide entertainment for everyone attending it, whether in the capacity of competitor or spectator, and this can only be done by careful and imaginative planning. Vast strides have been taken since those early days when the sport was in its infancy, and there can be no doubt that, as a sport in its own right, show jumping is here to stay. The thousands who flock to see it certainly appreciate the excitement and high standard of jumping provided by the international shows today.

Chapter Four

SHOW JUMPING

EVERYONE does not realize how much show jumping depends on the voluntary support of its public, who during the last five years have shown such increasing enthusiasm for the sport, and whose continually growing interest has encouraged the British team to reach its present high standard. Just after the war, our riders had had little experience of international show jumping and we were well below the standard of the foreign teams. In the speed competitions, we were laughed at because we had not trained our horses to jump at speed and turn quickly. Fortunately, there were great riders like Colonel Harry Llewellyn to make sure that we changed our methods. Then, with the leadership of Colonel M. P. Ansell behind the scenes, the team progressed from a Bronze Medal in the 1948 Olympic Games to the Gold Medal at Helsinki in 1952.

Even though we are now producing riders and horses to compete internationally, we cannot afford to sit back and relax. In 1954 at the White City we won the Nation's Cup, but the individual championship for the King George V Cup went to Germany. Another German rider won the World Championship. That country provided strong opposition also in the American shows, and they will certainly have a good team for the 1956 Olympic Games.

The French and Spaniards can always produce a strong team with good horses and plenty of international experience, and the Irish have some of the best horses in the world from which to choose. Every nation is improving, and even Russia will eventually find a team which can compete on equal terms with any of them. Before the war, Russia had great international riders. Although at Helsinki their team had not had sufficient experience, they will most certainly have learned a great deal from seeing the standard of the other riders.

We must always prepare young horses with the necessary boldness and freedom to enter for the supreme test of an Olympic course. Our well-known horses cannot last for ever in international jumping, for the physical and mental strain is very great when a horse is constantly facing big courses, and there are many difficulties that it may have to overcome.

Perhaps it may be tired after a long train or boat journey, or it may frighten and hurt itself on a fence if it makes a bad mistake when jumping. Quite often its legs will not stand the strain of continual jumping, galloping, and making quick turns. Or perhaps the nervous strain of competing in big competitions might become too much. It is then that the rider must know when to let it jump in an easy competition. On the other hand the horse may even need a rest or a complete change of environment.

This is not easy when abroad with a team, for the horses have been sent there to compete at the invitation of the country holding the show. Although the rider may know quite well that his horse is not absolutely fit on a certain day, he must still compete. That is just one of the risks. However, if a rider does retire from a competition when he feels that his horse is not up to the mark, although he may face the criticism of the public, he may at the same time save the confidence of his horse for the future. It is a decision which only the rider himself can make.

We have to prepare for the international jumping ahead bearing in mind any past mistakes. The first year the team went abroad was in 1947, and it went in the face of heavy

Col. Llewellyn on Foxhunter

opposition at home. The general opinion was that there was already plenty of jumping in this country, so why bother to go abroad?

Colonel Ansell has told elsewhere of the difficulty he had to convince the British Show Jumping Association that it was a worth-while venture, and how he eventually succeeded. When the question of finance was discussed at a Committee Meeting of seven, after the doubters had been persuaded, £170 in bank-notes were laid down upon the table in two minutes. From this encouraging beginning, a fund was launched and the members of the Association themselves subscribed £5,000. So a British team was able to go abroad.

The most important lesson learned that year was that we knew very little about the intricacies of the sport; in fact, the Swiss commented that we would do better on bicycles. But we came back with the determination to train our horses and riders to go abroad again—and win.

Another aspect of show jumping abroad which may not always be fully appreciated is the valuable trade it brings to this country. People from foreign countries come to England now in search of good horses, which they can buy and take home with them. And these are not just green horses, but the top-class horses trained here which have shown such good sport in the competitions abroad.

It is a mistake to think that the sport is becoming commercialized. Every big show in this country is run with the object of aiding the horse itself. The riders must work hard for their prize money and during a year the total income from such prizes very rarely exceeds three figures. Out of that, one has to keep the horses, costing at least three or four pounds a week each, travel the country paying one's own expenses and entrance fees, and when all the other incidental expenses have been met, there is very little left in the way of 'income'.

Finance is a problem which is constantly facing the B.S.J.A., because it costs so much money to send our teams abroad. The Olympic Fund of the B.S.J.A., at 66 Sloane Street, S.W.1, consists of voluntary subscriptions used for sending teams abroad to gain experience for

The British Team at the International Horse Show at White City, 1952. *Left to right:* Lt.-Col. H. M. Llewellyn on Foxhunter, Mr. W. White on Nizefela, Miss P. Smythe on Tosca, and Mr. P. Robeson on Craven A

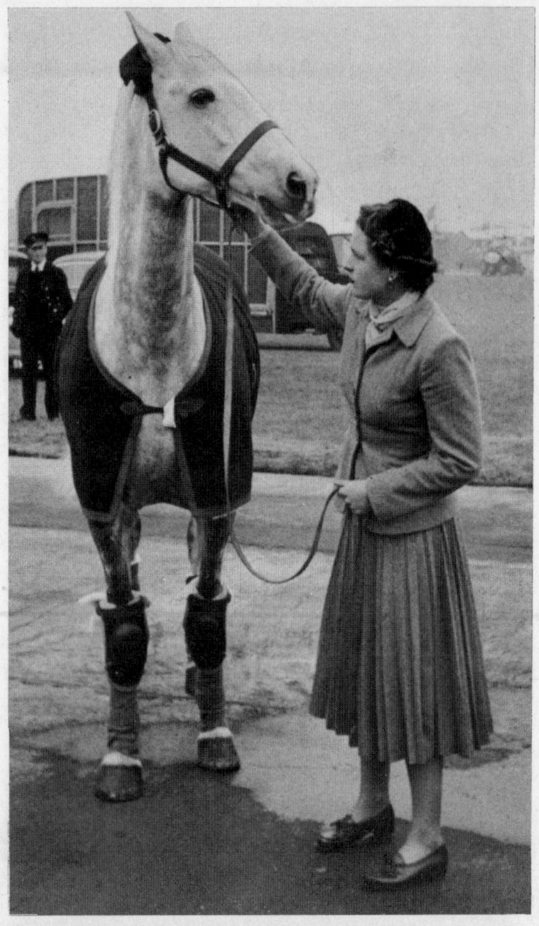

Tosca ready to leave in the plane for America. She is protected by a head-pad, bandages, and kneecaps

the Olympic Games. For instance, it would cost about £1400 to send a complete team of five riders and ten horses, with five grooms and a *chef d'équipe*, to the official international shows of Nice and Rome. These horses would travel both ways by rail and sea. However, when the Three-Day Event team went to compete at Basle, in Switzerland, it was essential that the horses should arrive in the peak of condition and fitness so they travelled by air. These four horses with one reserve and the four riders, *chef d'équipe*, and three grooms cost £1700 by the time they had returned by rail and sea.

Our American venture in 1953 was sponsored completely by voluntary subscriptions. It was essential that our horses should fly out to the States, not only so that they would arrive in good condition, but because there was only a week between our London show at Harringay and the first show on the American circuit at Harrisburg, Pennsylvania.

£3700 was needed to send a minimum team of six horses and three riders with no reserve. The required amount had still not been made up a week before we were due to leave, and then, after the Horse of the Year Show at Harringay, there was a letter in the *Daily Telegraph* which said there must have been many millions who had either seen the show on television, or heard it on the wireless, and the writer thought many of them would be only too pleased to contribute two shillings or half a crown for their evening's entertainment. As a result, the team was able to go and the many people who had contributed in this way took a personal interest in our achievements in the States.

When we go abroad we often receive support from home by telegram. Whenever Colonel Ansell sends us one, it nearly always ends with the words: 'Win, win and well, win.' It is this sort of encouragement, coupled with the knowledge that we are backed by the enthusiasm of people at home, that helps us on towards our victories.

I greatly appreciate these opportunities of going abroad and meeting the people of the various countries we visit, for I would never have had this chance to do so without show jumping. I know of no sport in which it is easier to make good friends with our 'neighbours' overseas, and I am sure that if there were more opportunity for travel and exchange of ideas there would never be so much international trouble. These visits abroad can be goodwill missions as much as anything else, and I am sure it is very worth while to learn something of the language of the country you are going to, even if you cannot manage a very convincing accent or achieve an extensive vocabulary. The people there appreciate your efforts, and it is far more interesting to be able to understand even a little than to make no attempt to join in any conversation.

The equestrian events in England at the moment are providing the public with very

Prince Hal winning the Grand Prix in Paris, 1954

Col. D. Stewart on Aherlow. The third member of our winning Olympic Team jumping at Dublin

exciting sport, especially with the county shows staging top-class jumping events. Also the smaller shows are improving the standard of their courses and so encouraging good jumping. It has been mainly through the public demand for the thrilling competitions under international rules that these courses have been improved, and it is from the agricultural and county shows that we draw our international jumpers of the future.

Since the war, too, other shows have been able to take a lead from the excellent organization and planning at the White City and Harringay, with better and more varied competitions producing jumping of a top-class standard.

Our riders have sometimes been criticized for not concentrating more on elementary dressage and the initial school training of our horses. This is easier to carry out in an indoor school, where the horse has no outside distractions to prevent it from concentrating. Unfortunately, we have very few covered schools available but we have far better facilities for training outdoors in the British Isles than some of the foreign countries, such as Switzerland and Sweden. Because of their hard winters they are obliged to concentrate on training their horses indoors. We can take our horses hunting, where they gain valuable experience jumping all types of fences. Horses and riding are still part of our life in the country, whereas abroad the riders do not have the same chance of hunting and amateur point-to-points, together with the Pony Club for the children. Even though we grumble about our weather, we can usually ride out-of-doors for most of the winter. This would be impossible at many places abroad, but in spite of having to train their horses indoors during the winter, these countries are great enthusiasts. It says much for their hard work in training under these difficulties that, together with Holland and Germany, they were at the forefront of the Olympic Games before the war.

It is impossible to achieve rapid results in training a horse for show jumping because of the great amount of preliminary work needed before it even sees a jump. When first ridden it has to adapt its whole balance to manage the unaccustomed weight of rider and saddle. Then it has to get used to the feeling of the bridle and saddle and accept the bit and the control through the reins. It must learn obedience from the rider and be made to concentrate on its work. While working it becomes more supple and builds up muscle like any athlete. It is not ready to start jumping until the rider has achieved willing co-operation by ordinary work at the walk, trot, and canter in the field. Even when the stage for jumping has been reached, one can always teach a horse to get over fences but that does not mean to say that it will ever make a show jumper. A horse with the necessary qualities to become a good show jumper needs the athletic ability and courage to jump huge fences, together with an ideal temperament and love of jumping. The horses that become stars in this sport are rare, and it is not easy to replace them.

Peter Robeson training Craven A at Aldershot before the 1952 Olympic Games

Alan Oliver on Red Admiral, winner of the National Championship in 1954

The young horses begin their training over small obstacles and so build up their confidence and ability. They must enjoy their work and gain the necessary practice and ability without becoming stale or bored. It is never wise to rush any stage of the training, or to take undue risks, because if the horse loses confidence it may then be necessary to start again right from the beginning. Some horses are much tougher than others and may not mind hitting a fence; in fact, they will often take more care over the next one. But the more sensitive ones may become frightened and lose their nerve if they touch a fence and hurt themselves. Then they must learn by stages to trust in their ability and discover for themselves that the job is not nearly so difficult and dangerous as they imagined.

After all this training the rider's problems have only just begun. The horse may turn out to lack that vital will to win when a crisis arises. It may fail to concentrate when jumping one of the fences or may just not bother to jump high enough. Sometimes it may not possess the nerve and temperament to face and overcome the risks involved. Those are the chances that one has to take.

Mr. Massarella's Costa, with Don Beard up, competing at Dublin in the high jumping

Yet all these past disappointments can disappear in a moment when you realize that the horse you are training can, with care and patience, become a top-class show jumper. It is a great pleasure to find a young horse improving with its training, and gradually making a name for itself. When the goal is reached, of winning a big event abroad, it gives one a feeling of having achieved something really worth while, surpassed only by the excitement of the competitions themselves and the intense effort required to get a win for one's country.

These competitions can also give one a humble attitude towards life. After the joy of a win one day, the following day the rider might quite easily find himself standing alone in the arena, bridle in hand, with the tail of his horse disappearing into the distance—the only proof of their recent successful partnership. It is very easy to fall off. Possibly the originator of the proverb 'Pride comes before a fall' had show jumping in mind when he thought of it.

The horses themselves react in different ways to the tenseness of the moment. As we stand awaiting our turn to go into the ring, Prince Hal flaps his lower lip, while Tosca invariably chews her bit. Some horses grind their teeth. They all have different ways of showing their nervous reaction and are quick to sense the atmosphere of the bigger competitions. Often when I am waiting to enter the ring, I can feel the horse's heart beating quickly between my knees, and sometimes it will tremble with excitement. For some horses the anticipation is too much and they refuse to go into the ring when it is their turn to jump the course. Some shows may bring back memories of a previous disaster or a fall. Then the horse may always connect that show with an unpleasant memory. Tosca had a bad fall and hurt herself in Rome, and after that experience she did not jump with her usual confidence in that arena.

If it had not been for Prince Hal's memory I might have won the Ladies' Competition in Brussels three years ago. The trouble came when we had to jump a fence of parallel bars at the end of the arena.

The night before, we had jumped a very similar obstacle in exactly the same position in a speed event. As we were about to land on the far side, I had turned Hal to the right so that we could negotiate the next obstacle without a second's delay. The following day, in the Ladies' Competition, we had to turn *left* after jumping this fence.

Hal had so far done a clear round and since the first round was not decided on time there was no great hurry. We cleared the parallel bars quite easily, and as we landed I began to turn left for the next obstacle. But Hal, remembering the speed and the lightning turn which had been necessary the previous evening, had already landed to the right in anticipation and as I was turning left I went straight round his neck. From this position I had to pull him up and struggle back into the saddle as quickly as possible, but although we finished with a clear round we forfeited a quarter of a time fault, and therefore did not qualify for the jump-off. On that occasion, Hal's memory was a little too good!

Another interesting example of a horse's memory concerned the renowned Galway Boy, which used to be jumped by Seamus Hayes but is now ridden by Alan Oliver. The first year the horse jumped at the Frome show in Somerset he had a very bad fall at a gate, laming himself for some time. It was a perfectly straightforward jump of the type one meets at any

Herr Thiedemann on Meteor at the White City, 1954, where he won the King George V Cup

Herr Winkler riding Halla, World Champion, 1954

show, but maybe Galway Boy had slipped as he took off. He has been to Frome each year since that accident but never once has he jumped the gate cleanly there, although he normally jumps a gate extremely well. He must remember his fall and therefore lacks confidence when he has to jump that same gate.

If there are a lot of obstacles in an arena, a horse will often try to choose for itself the one it thinks it would like to jump next, and begin to make its own arrangements to do so. It may perhaps make for the nearest one and I have even seen a horse jump enormous fences from the wrong side, ignoring the rider's frantic efforts to stop it. It is not easy for a rider to keep calm in speed events, so naturally the horse may get worked up. This is one of the reasons why it is so important for your horse to be obedient and respond immediately to your decisions. It is also vital that the rider should indicate as early as possible which way he wants the horse to go, so that it has ample warning and can react instantly. The sooner a horse can see the fence it is expected to jump, the less is the risk of its making a mistake and getting faults. A well-trained horse will be concentrating on each jump and its rider's guidance, whereas an inexperienced or badly trained horse may be fighting with its head against the rider's control, or looking at the lovely ladies in the crowd, and so be caught napping when it sees the next jump too late.

International competitions are judged in accordance with the regulations and rules of the Fédération Équestre Internationale. The horses are judged solely on their performance over the obstacles, and although the element of time enters into the judging of some competitions, the style of the horse and rider is not considered. There are three categories under

Wilf White jumping the White City water

which the competitions may be judged, and the category to be used for the particular competition is stated on the programme. These come under three headings, or 'tables'.

Table A. Penalty faults.

For each knock-down	4 faults
One or more feet in the water	4 faults
First refusal or disobedience	3 faults
Second refusal	6 faults
Third refusal	Elimination
Fall of horse or rider	8 faults

Faults for refusals accumulate throughout the whole course, which means that if a horse has a total of more than two it is eliminated. The speed required is given in the programme. The time allowed is calculated from this, and for each second or part of a second taken over this time the penalty is $\frac{1}{4}$ fault. There is a time limit in all competitions and this is twice the time allowed. If the competitor exceeds this, he is eliminated.

In Table A, the time element does not enter into the awards, except in the case of equality of faults when time may decide on the first round, or on the second or third, depending on the condition given in the programme. If the horses are equal in faults in this case, the horse which has finished the round in the fastest time is the winner. However, a slow clear round within the time allowed will always beat the fastest horse with faults.

Table B. This competition tests the speed and obedience as well as jumping capabilities. For each knock-down the competitor is penalized ten seconds. Refusals and falls are not penalized except that these waste the time taken by the competitor. The competitor who completes the course in the shortest time with the penalty seconds added is the winner. Therefore faults

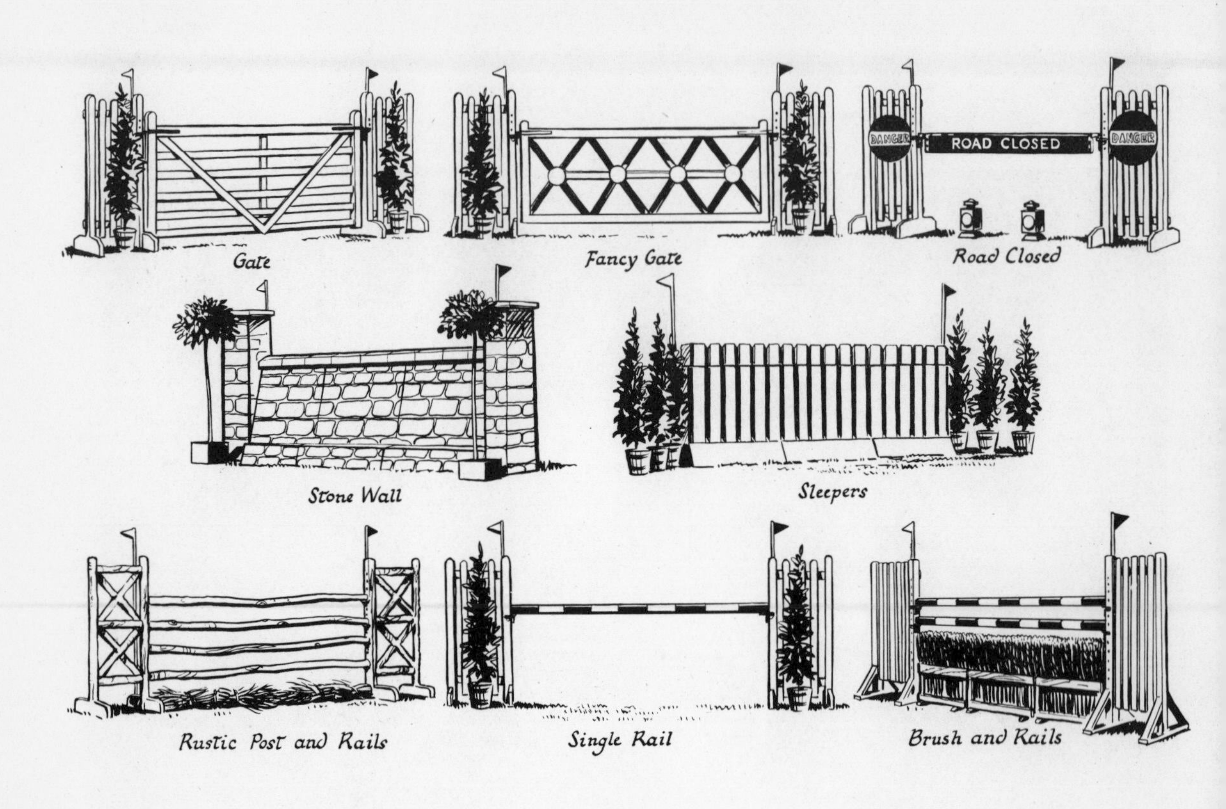
DANGER
ROAD CLOSED
DANGER
Gate
Fancy Gate
Road Closed
Stone Wall
Sleepers
Rustic Post and Rails
Single Rail
Brush and Rails

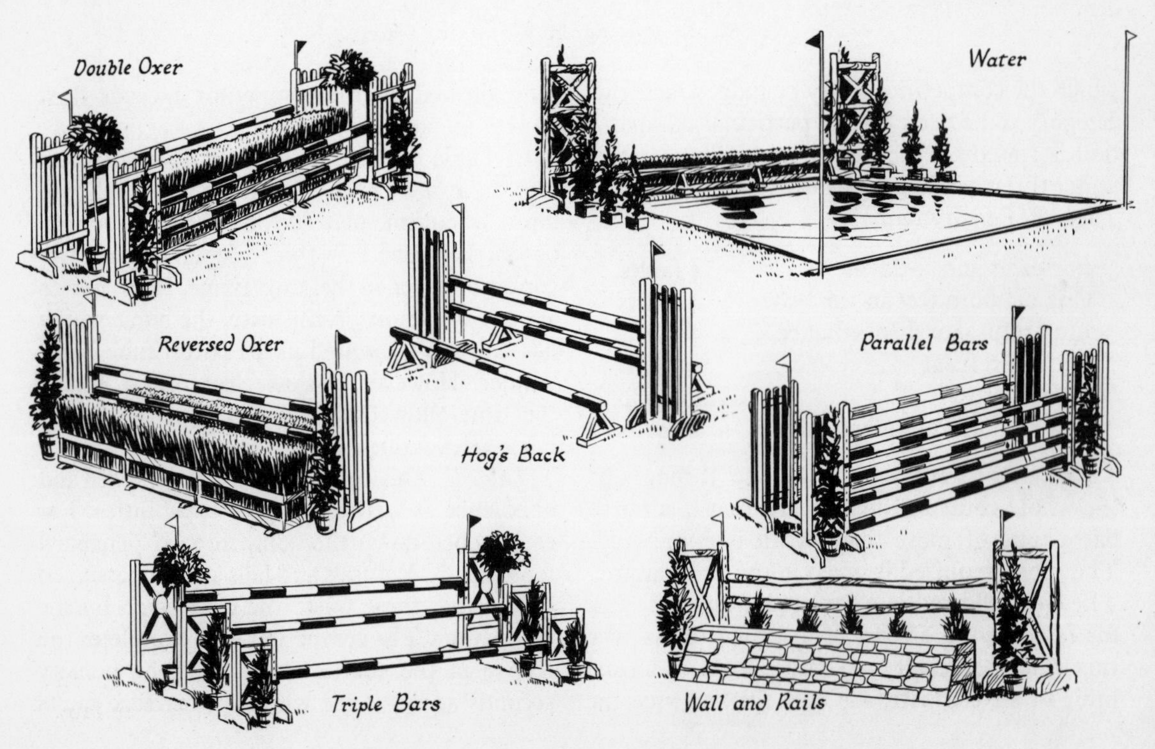
Double Oxer
Water
Reversed Oxer
Parallel Bars
Hog's Back
Triple Bars
Wall and Rails

Edward Prince of Wales Cup—2.25 p.m. Thursday, 22nd July, 1954
(PRIX DES NATIONS)

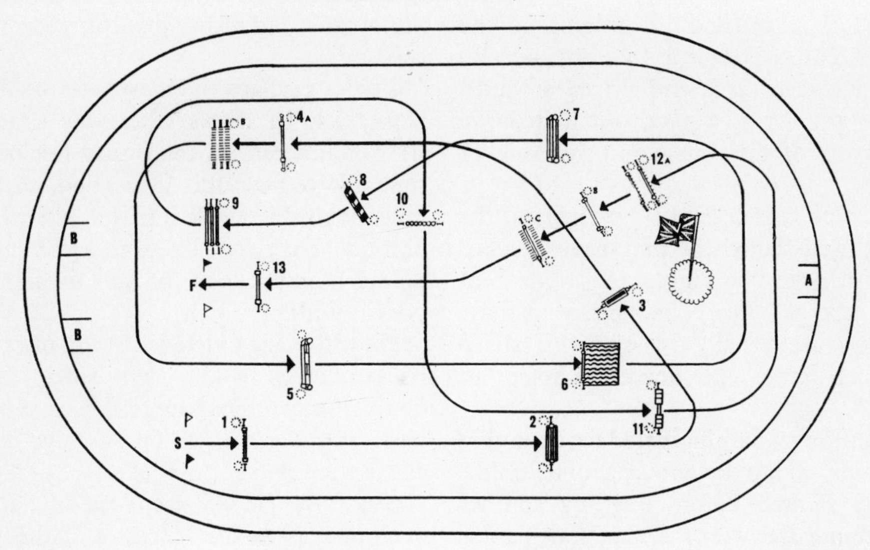

FENCES
1. Brush and Rails.
2. Hogs Back.
3. Water Trough.
4. A Double.
   (a) Brush and Rail.
   (b) Triple of Brush.
5. Red Wall.
6. Water.
7. Yellow Wall.
8. Sleepers.
9. Triple Bar.
10. Log Wall.
11. Gloucestershire Stile.
12. A Treble.
   (a) Parallel Poles.
   (b) Red Pillars and Rails.
   (c) Reversed Oxer.
13. White Gate.
A. Bandstand.
B. Entrance from Collecting Ring.
S. Start.
F. Finish.

King George V Gold Challenge Cup—9.10 p.m. Wednesday, 21st July, 1954
(FINAL)

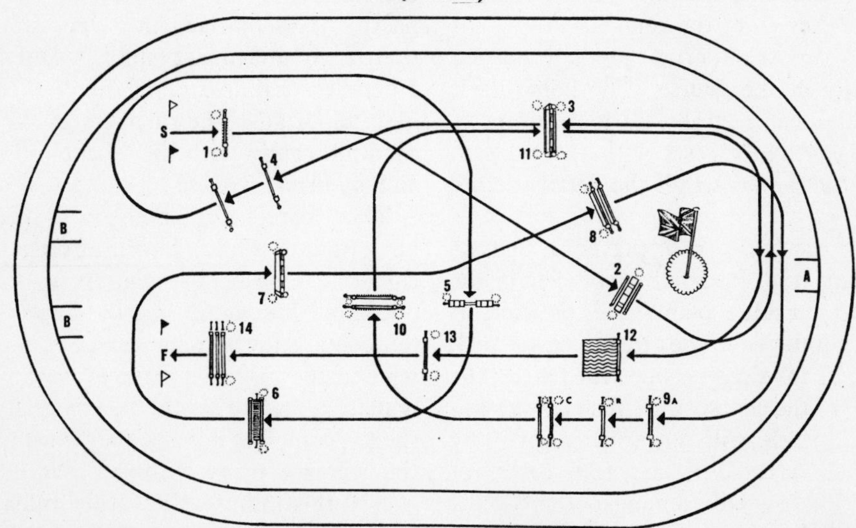

FENCES
1. Brush and Rail.
2. The Bridge.
3. Yellow Wall.
4. A Double.
   (a) Railway Crossing Gate.
   (b) Railway Crossing Gate.
5. Gloucestershire Stile.
6. Double Oxer.
7. Red Wall.
8. Parallel Poles.
9. A Treble.
   (a) Single Rail.
   (b) Single Rail.
   (c) Parallel Poles.
10. Parallel Poles.
11. Yellow Wall.
12. Water.
13. White Gate.
14. Triple Bar.
A. Bandstand.
B. Entrance from Collecting Ring.
S. Start.
F. Finish.

are not given as they are converted into penalty seconds.

Table C. This method of judging is the same as in Table B except that the penalty may vary between three and fifteen seconds. The actual penalty is worked out in relation to the distance of the course and the number of obstacles.

In the Table B and Table C categories, the fast horse, even though he may have knocked down one or even two fences, will often beat the slow, careful horse. The courses in these competitions are usually twisty, with sharp turns, which gives the obedient horse an advantage.

A competitor can be eliminated for a number of reasons: for taking the wrong course, unless he corrects himself before jumping another fence; jumping the wrong fence; starting his round before the signal has been given to start; showing his horse a fence when waiting to start or while waiting for a fence to be rebuilt after a refusal; receiving unauthorized assistance; or leaving the ring voluntarily or involuntarily, before completing a round.

So there is plenty for both rider and horse to think about! But there is always a lot to be done even before they enter the ring.

The rider's most important job is to make a careful study of the course. The horse itself never sees the fences until it starts to jump, so a great responsibility rests with the rider to make sure that he knows all the details before they start.

A plan of the course is displayed in or near the collecting ring. It should show clearly the starting and finishing points, the position of each fence numbered in the order to be jumped, the track to be followed between the fences, the total length of the course, the time allowed and the time limit. It will not usually give any particulars about the type, structure, or size of the fences. These details, amongst others, must be noted by the rider when he inspects the course later on.

This plan gives the rider a golden opportunity of learning by heart the way round, so that he has no doubt which fence follows which and knows instinctively the route to be taken and each change of direction. Having made a thorough study of the plan, he then walks the course.

This is perhaps the most vital of all the preliminaries. In shows where the time-table is strictly adhered to, there may not be a lot of time allowed for this inspection, so the rider must be ready to walk into the ring the moment permission is given. There are a great number of points he must look for and memorize as he goes round.

He will make a detailed study of each fence, its structure, height, and width, and (with doubles or combinations of fences) the distance between the jumps, to find out the number of strides the horse must take to negotiate them successfully. He will study the line and length of approach to the fences, and the points at which he can save time by jumping at an angle. For speed events, the rider will notice which fences are likely to impress his horse more than others, and the places where it would be unwise to take a risk by turning too short. The position of any turning flags must be carefully studied to ensure that one passes them on the correct side. In fact, a great deal of information has to be memorized in a very short time—there is no time to make notes!—and that is why a detailed examination of the plan beforehand is so important. The rider enters the arena for his walk round with the 'shape' of the course already firmly fixed in his mind.

Then comes the moment to prepare the horse for its round. It will already have been ridden to make sure that it is supple and obedient. Inevitably it will sense the rider's tenseness and become tensed up itself, but once in the ring they have to wait for the bell which indicates that the jury is ready to judge them. As soon as it rings, they must go through the starting posts within a minute. If they exceed this minute, they are eliminated. Once through the start they face the first jump, which is usually a fairly easy one to allow the horse to get balanced and gain confidence.

Then on to the more complicated obstacles, where the horse and rider must prove their partnership, unaware of the hushed stillness of the crowd or the sudden bursts of applause as each fence is cleared. For nothing matters now but the course ahead. Everything depends on their performance during less than two minutes in the ring. The powers of concentration, firmness, and sympathy must come into play, with the rider prepared to ask the impossible, yet so convincingly that his horse responds to his every command, obedient and confident.

At last comes the moment to relax, when the clock stops as he cuts the finishing line after the last fence. Then, as he walks his horse from the arena, if the roar of the crowd acclaims a clear round, he knows that his hard work and patience have been amply rewarded. It is a glorious moment for them both.

Prince Hal winning the Puissance in Algiers, April 18th 1955. This fence was raised again before he finally beat the German horse Halla

Chapter Five

HUNTING

WE are very lucky in Great Britain to have many famous Hunts and some of the best hunting country in the world. It is a mistake, however, to think that because a horse is a brilliant hunter it will necessarily make a good show jumper. A hunter, used to the company and excitement of a hunt, will often dislike the completely different atmosphere of the show ring, and will see very little point in jumping man-made fences in cold blood after the joy of jumping across country to the cry of hounds.

That is the reason I like to begin my young horses over show fences and take them hunting afterwards. Then they make ideal hunters because they have learned to jump properly and enjoy it. After a spell of hunting I hope to take them show jumping again because, with the additional experience gained across country, they will have learned to look after themselves when jumping strange fences.

At first it is much better for a young horse to go out alone across country away from the bewildering throng of the hunt. In this way, it learns to think individually and to take the fences calmly. In addition, you can choose your own obstacles to train over and will not incur the wrath of the farmers by damaging their property, since you will be making sure that your jumping is accurate.

A day's hunting is the most satisfying way I know of spending one's leisure. Unfortunately, I rarely get enough chance nowadays because there is always so much else to do, but at one time I was able to hunt almost every day during the season. Sometimes we had to do the house shopping first because groceries could not be delivered in the country. This meant being at the shops by nine o'clock in the morning in order to be back to start off for the meet at ten!

Even today there are quite a lot of personal matters to be attended to before a day's hunting, such as housekeeping problems and letters to be answered, because we shall probably not be home again before the post goes.

Most of the actual preparations before hunting can be done the night before. The tack is cleaned and polished, and my boots are boned to make the grain of the leather lie flat before being polished. My coat and breeches are brushed as soon as they are dry after the last day's hunting. Often the breeches have to be washed and scrubbed after a very muddy day, or if one happened to have a fall and 'buy a bit of land', that tell-tale green stain on the seat of the breeches must be removed!

Hunting boots are not the same as those we use for show jumping and point-to-points. They have to be much stronger to stand the wear and tear of the hunting field, with the reverse side of the leather to the outside so that any scratches can be boned down. The bone is usually a deer shank and, if it is properly used, all the scratches can be worked out of the leather. Then with a little elbow grease the boots can be polished up to look like patent leather. Show jumping boots are much lighter in weight and more comfortable to walk about in. The natural shiny side of the leather is on the outside, the same as with a shoe, so that a good polish makes the surface shine brilliantly. They are never boned.

The night before hunting, the horses are given a good feed. They do not get much hay because they will not want too much bulk inside them with fast exercise the following day. On

Hounds arriving at a meet in Sussex

The V. W. H. Bathurst Hunt moving off after a meet at Wings School

the morning of the meet, they have a small hard feed early and are then groomed. Their manes are plaited up and tails bandaged. As much care should be taken over the appearance of the horses as your own. It is a point of respect and politeness to the Master of the pack with whom you are hunting, to turn out as smartly as possible.

As soon as I am ready I put on an old coat and fetch the lorry, which is kept about half a mile from the house. In the very cold weather we always drain the radiator to prevent it from freezing up, so after half filling it from a bucket of hot water I start to crank the engine. Sometimes it starts easily, sometimes it does not. In any case, it is a very good way of warming yourself up on a cold winter's morning. Having got the box started and to the stables, I finish filling up the radiator. Fresh straw is put down on the floor of the box and the hay nets are filled ready for the horses to eat after the day's hunting. They are never given anything to eat on the way to the meet. When they are bridled and saddled, a rug is put over the saddle and a head collar over the bridle. Then they are ready to be loaded into the box.

If we are off for a day's show jumping the tack is never put on the horses, because there is usually a long journey to the show. The journey to the meet, however, is normally quite short so they can travel in their bridles and saddles. After collecting my cap, whip, and hunting coat from the house, we are ready to start.

Before we get to the meet, I try to find a vantage point to park the box, preferably somewhere out of the way but on the side that the hunt may finish up. Normally, hounds will work towards kennels during the evening, although it is never certain where they will finish at the end of the day. The horses are then unloaded and ridden the final part of the journey to the meet. This should settle them down so that they arrive in a sane frame of mind! A fit hunter usually starts the day very much on its toes.

If the Master is there, the first thing one should do is to greet him with: 'Good morning, Master.' The next thing is to see the Hunt Secretary and pay the wire fund money, which is paid each time in addition to the yearly subscription to the Hunt. With still a few minutes to spare before the hounds move off, there is time to greet friends and to have a word or two about the prospects of the day with one of the Hunt servants. It is interesting to see how many hounds are out that day, and they are always counted in couples, with an odd number comprising the pack, usually about eighteen and a half couple. If the meet is taking place at a private house, there may be some sandwiches or a glass of port offered by the host. When the Master is ready, he moves off followed by hounds, with the whipper-in bringing up the rear of the pack to make sure that there are no stragglers.

Sometimes the Master's place will be taken by a huntsman, who can be an amateur or a professional Hunt servant. This could occur when the Master is unable to hunt hounds himself. Although the Master backs the Hunt financially, he may prefer to follow hounds with the rest of the field. In that case, he would engage a professional huntsman to hunt hounds and it is the huntsman who is responsible for the sport shown.

Another very important person is the Field Master, who, as his name implies, is responsible for the behaviour of the field, or the followers of the Hunt. It is his job to see that they do not ride over wheat or do damage to the farmers' fences or fields. He must also watch to see that the field does not override hounds and so spoil the chances of picking up a catchy scent. Then the field must stand in the right place by a covert to let the fox get away.

So the Master leads off to the first draw and puts hounds into covert. The field waits quietly away from the side where the fox should break. A person is stationed inconspicuously at a corner of the covert, or at some other vantage point so that he can watch for the fox. As soon as the fox finds that hounds are making it too hot for it to stay in covert, it will break away. When the person watching views the fox, he waits until it has got well away and then he rides over to the place where it left the covert. Then he can give a 'holloa' and raise his hat above his head. The field wait until they hear the huntsman blow the 'gone away' on the horn, and then they can gallop to the holloa, and if hounds are not already on the line they must wait until they break covert. Usually hounds come tumbling out together and take up the line at once. Then, and only then, may the field follow. As soon as hounds get on to the scent of a fox they start to give tongue, and if the scent is very strong they burst into music. This is the sound that is so exciting to hear, thrilling both horses and riders alike.

The fox normally breaks away with the wind so that its scent is not carried back to the pack, but if it knows that an earth lies in the opposite direction, it might very well make for it, and try to go to ground there.

Sometimes hounds will lose the scent and a check will follow. This may happen if the fox runs through cattle or sheep or swims a stream. It may go through a field recently fertilized with artificial fertilizers, which will not hold scent. Then the Master has to make a 'cast' by taking hounds in a large circle around that area until they hit the line again. While this is happening, the field usually waits, although if the Master is making a wide cast they may follow him behind the Field Master. As soon as one hound picks up the scent again, it gives tongue, and the others join it if they have found the line, and away they go.

When jumping, great care should always be taken not to damage the farmers' fences. With a field of two or three hundred, immense gaps can be made by everyone queueing up to jump in the same place. Ideally, of course, everybody should be capable of jumping without hitting the fences at all, but although they may have

The Duke of Beaufort with his hounds at White City

the necessary courage, the horses or riders may lack knowledge and experience. Very often one takes on a fence without knowing what lies on the other side, then there is always a risk that it might be wired. Most good farmers mark the places which are safe to jump, and for this purpose they use stakes surmounted by plaques. A white one indicates there is no wire, but if the fence is wired the places where it is safe to jump are marked with a plaque which is white on the side to be jumped and red on the wired side of the fence. A fence with no jumping place has a plain red plaque.

A horse keeps in better condition if it does not do more than half a day's hunting, say, from eleven until one or two in the afternoon. This will naturally depend on the amount of sport shown, but when it is tired the horse should be cooled off and taken back to the box. The girth is loosened and its rug is put on to keep it warm, like an athlete putting on a sweater after a race. If you are lucky enough to have a second horse, the groom will try to meet you so that you can change horses and carry on with the sport. He must have a good idea which way hounds are running and follow them as best he can by going the shortest way on the roads. It is essential that your second horse should be fresh when you change on to it to continue the day. Though it has been known that a groom was carried away with the excitement of the sport, and galloped side by side with his master, and then at the appointed hour for changing horses, he solemnly got off his steaming horse and held it while his employer climbed aboard. The discarded horse again joined the chase, with the groom taking on all fences that came between himself and hounds!

When riding a horse back to its box after the hunt, it should be walked for the last part of the way to let it cool off, both mentally and physically, otherwise it will still be sweating when you put the rug on. When in the box, the bridle comes off and the head collar and rug go on. It helps to dry the horse off if the saddle stays on under the rug. It is then given its hay net and, when cooled off, can have some warm water to drink. If it is tired or exhausted, a pint or two of beer in its water bucket will help it to relax and calm down.

On arriving home the horse should be unloaded immediately and taken to the stable. If it is very tired, a thorough grooming to remove all the mud can wait until later. Its heels must be absolutely dry since otherwise they might become cracked. Loose bandages round the legs will help them to dry off. By then it is ready for its first feed. This is a bran mash with linseed which is easy to digest and acts as a laxative. Later we may give a hard feed depending on the work to be done the next day. In any case, a horse does not need much work on the day after hunting, although it is a good thing to walk it out to remove any stiffness. After hunting, it is important to see that the horse is kept warm and is not shivering from excitement or showing any signs of exhaustion. The rider must be sure that his horse is comfortable and being well looked after before he goes off for his own tea and a hot bath.

Etiquette in the hunting field is something you begin to learn in the Pony Clubs. There is nothing worse than a display of bad manners from one of the followers. One of the first things to remember is that hounds take first place over everything and everybody. There can never be any excuse for impeding them in their job or getting in their way. Should a hound get left behind and want to get through a gateway, the field must stand aside and let it pass. The Master will usually not go home until all his hounds have been collected together. If by mischance one of them is lost, the Master might take the rest of the pack home and come out in his car later to find it. A hound can never be left out all night because of the danger of traffic on our roads.

A Master looks after his hounds like children, but this is not always the case when hunting abroad. In fact, the general attitude of foreigners towards hunting often appears rather unorthodox to anyone who has hunted in Great Britain.

Not so long ago I had a day out with a drag hunt abroad. My first surprise was to find that the pack of five and a half couple were really coupled—round their necks—and hounds were not let loose by the huntsman until just before they arrived at the meet. This, I believe, was because of the difficulty in controlling them. The first mishap occurred after the drag was laid. Hounds found a scent of real fox and went off on it. In England, one always follows hounds wherever they go, so off I galloped after them into the scrub. They were hunting well and we were all enjoying ourselves thoroughly, but after about an hour they lost the scent and stood about uncertainly, not quite sure what to do about it. I turned round expecting to find the huntsman nearby ready to cast them, but to my dismay discovered I was entirely on my own. Neither Master, huntsman, nor field were in sight. I could not imagine where they had got to. There was only one thing to do, so I tried to get hounds to follow me and started to hack back to the point where I thought the meet had been, trusting to my memory of the landmarks to get me back safely.

Fortunately, my memory did not fail me and as I approached the meet I came upon a very sorrowful sight. The Master and several members of the field were riding up and down looking very cold and disconsolate, and I could not understand why until he rode up to me and cried: 'Where ever have you been? What a relief! We thought you'd got lost in the bush. We even rang up to see if you'd gone home.' Everyone seemed to have forgotten about hounds and were surprised when I said that I had been following them. Their great concern was what had happened to me. I looked round and saw the rest of the field still standing at the start of the drag. No one had made any attempt to follow hounds, presumably because they had come out for a drag hunt and nothing other than a drag hunt would interest them—not even the scent of real fox.

At last, however, we started off on the drag. All went well until the pack split on a fresh fox scent. The field split too, half on the drag line and half on the fox line, scattering in all directions. For a time the rival parties went out of sight, but eventually the two lines crossed and we were reunited in a vast wood—hounds and all. By now, the Master decided he had had enough and that we should go home. I offered to help in collecting up hounds, but he waived my suggestion aside saying that they were quite capable of finding their own way home. I could not believe my ears at first, but obviously he meant what he said, because without further ado he set off for home leaving the hounds to fend for themselves. Someone told me that it was too difficult to collect them in such a large forest. However, I managed to gather two and a half couple together and took them home with me. Some of the others did not get home for two days. It was certainly a most amusing day's hunting with a true pioneer spirit.

In Canada, where they enjoy their sport immensely, they treat it far more like a social event than we do. There is usually a big hunt breakfast immediately afterwards, when all the followers can talk over the excitements of their day's sport. These are always extremely enjoyable, and the Canadians are exceptionally hospitable people, but I must admit that I do like a hot bath after hunting before a large meal. The cold can be intense there, and of course the hunting season is very short with the winter closing down before Christmas.

Another point of etiquette which may at first confuse the newcomer to the hunting field is the traditional 'Good-night' one gives to the Master at the end of the day, even if you are finishing in the middle of the afternoon. Similarly if one decided to go home at any time, possibly two o'clock, this is still the correct way to bid farewell to the Master or, if he is not in the immediate vicinity, to one's friends nearby.

Children should never push in front of grown-ups when negotiating a gateway or obstacle. This should apply to all walks of life, of course, not only in the hunting field, but unfortunately one still sees these occasional displays of bad manners. Never cross a field of wheat or growing crops. It is essential to ride only around the edge of a field that is sown but it is usually possible to avoid jumping into a wheat field.

After a long run, which has ended in the country of a neighbouring Hunt, the Master has to take hounds back to his own country before he can make another draw. This is another point of etiquette which is always strictly observed. So long as hounds find in their own country it does not matter if the kill takes place across a border, but it is poaching to stay there for the next draw. It might seem an unnecessarily long trek back, but it is obviously unfair to 'steal' foxes from one's neighbours.

I can remember being involved once in one of these long rides to the next draw, but on that occasion I never reached it.

I had hacked over to the meet about eight miles from Miserden on a thoroughbred mare called Tudor Rose. Hounds found immediately and went away very fast, eventually running into the neighbouring Bathurst country. During the run we had to cross a river, which gradually deepened into about three feet of water, and climb up the bank on the far side. We negotiated this successfully on the way out but coming back I was not so lucky.

After hounds had killed their fox up on Bibury aerodrome, we had to turn back for the next draw into our own country. It was a considerable way off. As we came to the river again my horse, instead of clambering down the bank and walking out the far side, decided it would be much easier to jump into the middle of the river. She was quite wrong, because she went straight under and disappeared to the bottom. And there I sat, my legs still astride a horse which none could see.

The field was small that day and they all roared with laughter, to see me sitting in the middle of the river, making swimming motions. But it was not very funny for poor Tudor Rose, who was struggling frantically to get up from the bottom of the river. At last she managed it without falling on her side and, dripping wet, we clambered up the bank. It took a little time to calm her down before I was able to discover what had happened, and then to my dismay I found she had lost a shoe. As she landed in the river she must have caught her foot between two roots, and pulled the shoe off while trying to get free. It was certainly a sorry situation. Twenty-two miles from home, a horse with only three shoes, a bitterly cold wind blowing, and both of us soaking wet. There would be no more hunting for us that day.

We hacked back with hounds to our own country, where they immediately found a fox, and, very fed up with ourselves, we watched the field gallop off. Tudor Rose and I trudged home, she going clipperty plonk and me with the water squelching in my boots.

Different types of country require different types of horses for successful hunting. In my own country, the Cotswold, you need a horse which jumps high to clear the stone walls. These walls have sharp-edged coping stones on top and a knee cut from one of them can very quickly turn poisonous, and the result can take a very long time to heal. As a contrast, the Leicestershire country needs the thoroughbred type of horse which can gallop over the big fields and will jump freely. Here there are ditches both towards and away from the fences, and it needs a bold horse to have the pace and ability to jump out the other side. If a fence has a ditch each side one needs a very free jumping horse.

In Ireland a horse gets used to jumping banks. Over a good bank the horse should jump to the top, but a clever horse will always know where to put his feet. Or if the bank is narrow, he might not touch it in front at all but jump it with an extra kick back with his hind legs. When they first come to England, Irish horses often try to change legs on top of fences thinking they are banks. Similarly, a horse accustomed to jumping fly fences would have no idea how to negotiate banks.

Therefore, it is always easier, when hunting with a strange pack in unknown country, to ride a horse which knows the country.

I had another rather unusual day's hunting while staying abroad when I went out with the local Hunt. After a long run, a fox we had been hunting went under a chicken house and hounds lost the scent. The Master was waiting on the other side of the field, across the middle of which was a deep bog. The fox suddenly came out from its hiding place and was chopped immediately.

The Master was so excited that he galloped across the field and went straight into the bog. Undeterred, he abandoned his horse, hat, and whip in the middle of it and, floundering up the other side, seized the dead fox. The field gathered round expectantly as the Master took hold of a knife and began to cut off the fox's limbs to give them as trophies of the chase.

By this time hounds had lost interest and instead of waiting eagerly to break up the fox, as they do here, most of them had wandered off and were nosing amongst the rubbish bins in a nearby farm. One or two had stayed behind, so the Master threw the remains of the fox to them. They sniffed it suspiciously, looked at each other, and then walked away in disgust. Perhaps they so rarely killed a fox, they had not acquired the taste.

I was very interested in the American hounds and astounded at the number of packs they have all down the Eastern Seaboard—from New England to North Carolina. Many of the hounds are English bred but there is also a strain of American hounds that they have developed to suit their conditions. I was intrigued by the famous Orange County hounds in Virginia which live up to the colour of their county and look most attractive.

The Americans are famous for their ingenious gadgets which are practical and labour saving. In one kennels, an American huntsman had made good use of his initiative. He lived in a flat above the kennels and his sleep was disturbed on clear nights when hounds came out into the yard to howl at the moon. So one morning, after a couple of sleepless nights and the weather set fair with the moon at its zenith, he had an idea.

He had just had a new bath installed in his

flat, and the large shower that the plumbers had left would not fit in his tiny bathroom. So he fixed this shower in the hound yard. Then he arranged the remote control with a bell push in his bedroom. When the moon rose that night, inducing hounds out into the yard to voice their emotions, the huntsman turned over in bed, put his finger on the bell push, and the shower started up in the yard. The hounds thought that it was raining so they went back to bed. Peace reigned once more under the silvery moon.

Hunting gets into the blood, and that is why packs have been started, often under very difficult conditions, all over the world. But it is these Isles that have always been the home of fox hunting.

One should add a word about cars following hounds. Today, the cars have become as big a menace as wire, and they can spoil not only our sport but their own as well. A hunt can be ruined when they 'head' the fox. The defence of one offending motorist who had committed this unforgivable sin was, 'Oh well, I only diverted it'!

When a motorist finds himself in front of hounds, it is better to pull up and keep very still, by a stack, shed, or thick fence, rather than in the open. Then he may see 'Charlie' cross over and have a wonderful view of all the hunt.

Some Grove and Rufford hounds waiting expectantly at kennels

Chapter Six

THE THREE-DAY EVENT AT BADMINTON

In the old horse-cavalry days, tests to try out the all-round capabilities of their chargers were carried out regularly by the officers of every army in Europe. These nearly always included an endurance test, a test across country, and jumping and riding-school tests. To begin with, they were more in the nature of private and personal events, when every officer wanted to make sure that his own charger was well trained and able to get him out of a tight corner if necessary. Gradually, however, they became more organized and competitive, until eventually they took a definite shape in the form of three distinct phases usually run on separate days: a dressage test; a cross-country and endurance test; and a jumping test.

In 1912, with the introduction of equestrian events into the Olympic Games, one of these competitions was included. It became known as the 'Three-Day Event'.

Until quite recently, our British teams had little success in the competitions. At Stockholm in 1912 we failed to complete the course, and at Paris twelve years later we finished sixth. We did not compete again until 1936 at Berlin when, in spite of collecting many time penalties owing to a runaway horse after a fall, all three members of the team completed the course and gained third place. In 1948 the Games were held in London, and we were one of the eleven nations eliminated. The winners were U.S.A., with Sweden second.

Our team that year was the last all-military one to represent England. Today, thanks to the vision and initiative of the Duke of Beaufort, who allows an annual Olympic horse trial to take place at his home, Badminton, our chances in the international events improve year by year, and we now have a good selection of young riders and horses from which to draw our teams.

The trials at Badminton began in 1949 and since then the sport has grown considerably in popularity. Smaller replicas of the contest in the shape of one-day events take place every year all over the country, watched by hundreds of spectators who have been quick to appreciate their interest and appeal.

The Duke of Beaufort's lovely estate at Badminton in Gloucestershire is an ideal setting for the Three-Day Event. The arena is laid out in front of the big house against an enchanting background of trees and parkland. There is ample car space for spectators and plenty of room for the competitors' horses, which are accommodated in luxury in the Beaufort Hunt stables. Some of the competitors themselves stay at the 'Hare and Hounds' at Westonbirt, an appropriately named hostelry!

The first day at Badminton is devoted to dressage, the second to an endurance test, and the third to show jumping. The same horse is used on each day, and the purpose of the competition is to show that one horse is capable of carrying out each of these three distinct phases of training. In French, the word for a horse which is trained for the three-day competition is *concours complet*, meaning the 'complete' horse for this event, and thus we have to rely on the French to find the phrase which conjures up so precisely the picture of the perfect, well-trained horse.

Major Weldon on Kilbarry doing his dressage test at Badminton during the Olympic Horse Trials

Dressage occupies the whole of the first day. Each horse is in the arena for approximately ten minutes, with the test itself lasting about eight minutes. The test is designed to prove the suppleness and complete obedience of the horse to the rider, without loss of freedom of action and movement. It is also a severe test of concentration, and during the time they are in the arena neither rider nor horse must allow any distraction to upset them. This is not easy when the horse is feeling very fit—as it must in order to cope with the subsequent phases.

To many people, the word 'dressage' is something of a mystery, but in actual fact the methods used today have always been used subconsciously by many of the best natural horsemen in the country. It is merely that now this form of obedience training has been given a name and an attempt has been made to describe the correct way to perform each movement. One of the objects is to explain and teach the methods employed by the experts, for unless he had studied equitation, a good horseman, when asked how he made his horse carry out a particular movement, would probably be unable to describe exactly how it was done.

Dressage is divided into two categories: Classical and Field dressage. The former is used only by those who want to train their horses for advanced dressage and the High School. For this the rider must be an advanced horseman and must be ready to give up a lot of his time to the art. He cannot afford to use his horse for anything else, since he obviously could not risk injuring it in day-to-day field work after spending so much time on its special training.

Field dressage, on the other hand, benefits every riding horse which is required for field work, whether this be hunting, show jumping, combined training, hacking, polo, or, to a certain extent, racing. With a little help from an expert it can be practised by any reasonably good horseman, and is in fact nothing more than the type of training taught in the military schools of the past and used in the training of cavalry remounts.

There is nothing new or mysterious about dressage. Two hundred years ago the great French horseman, La Guérinière, on whose doctrines and teachings the leading riding schools of Europe base the principles of their instruction, wrote in his book: 'The aim of training the horse is to make him quiet, supple, and obedient by systematic work so that he becomes pleasant in his movements and comfortable for his rider. This applies in exactly the same way to the hunter, the charger, or the school horse.'

A course of systematic field dressage is vitally necessary for every riding horse, and particularly the jumper. Not only does it develop the mental and physical abilities, but it also insures against undue strain on sinews and muscles before they are ready. To begin with, the horse is asked to carry out only the most simple exercises, and then taken by stages on to the more difficult ones, so that neither its physical strength nor its intelligence is overstrained. The final outcome of this training is that it grows accustomed to authority, always keeps calm, and acquires the habit of instant obedience.

Today, with the increase in the standard of jumping, this training is essential for the jumper, whose degree of obedience, physical fitness, and ability to change direction quickly are the main factors contributing to success in the show ring. There is no doubt that since we began to study and concentrate on this basic training in this country, our standard of jumping has improved considerably.

The second day at Badminton is the most important, and the most strenuous, when the horses are put through an endurance test. This takes place over roads and tracks, a steeplechase course, and a cross-country course, covering in all about 17 miles.

The first phase over roads and tracks has to be completed in a given time, although no bonus points are awarded for finishing the course under that time. Therefore, it has to be ridden at exactly the right pace, and success depends on the precision of the rider's judgment. The steeplechase course which follows is the one used by the Beaufort Hunt Point-to-Point, although for the Three-Day Event competitors only ride one round instead of the usual two circuits when taking part in a point-to-point. Also, at Badminton, two made-up fences are erected at the finish of the course. For this test, time does count and a rider who finishes in a fast time receives many bonus points. On the other hand, unless a horse is able to jump steeplechase fences at speed, it is not worth risking a fall by trying to push it along too fast. Not only are many points forfeited for a fall, but there is always the added risk of injury.

Miss M. Hough on Bambi V leaves the Dragon's Lair during the Harewood Three-Day Event

Neptune jumping the bank at Badminton during the Cross-Country phase

After this course there is another spell over roads and tracks. Again, these have to be covered in a given time. This phase also gives the horse a good opportunity to calm down after its gallop over the steeplechase obstacles. On arrival at the beginning of the cross-country run, competitors are allowed about two minutes' rest providing, of course, they arrive on time. This break gives the rider just sufficient time to dismount, adjust the saddle, and swill out the horse's mouth with water. He may also freshen it by putting a wet sponge over its ears and eyes, and possibly give it a lump of sugar to bolster up its energy. Then he must be up again and ready to start the cross-country.

Once more, in this phase every second is vital and a great number of bonus points can be gained by a fast round. Nevertheless, great care has to be taken to avoid mistakes, for many points can be lost through falls, running out, or refusals. Falls are very heavily penalized and a horse is allowed only four refusals at any one obstacle before it is eliminated.

Although none of the fences is higher than four foot, they are very solid and it needs a bold horse to jump them without falling. It may have to tackle an obstacle from muddy going, or over a six-foot ditch in front of the fence. There are often big drops on the landing side, and to the horse it may seem as though

Carmena jumping the famous Coffin at Badminton

it is jumping into space. At one point it has to jump over a small fence and down a slide into a quarry, and although this is not so difficult if the horse tackles it sensibly, some of them are rather over-awed and frightened by it.

There are also doubles and trebles on the course. One of these entails jumping out of a field into a drop lane, up on to a bank, and then straight over a post-and-rails. Here again, it is not a particularly difficult obstacle as long as the horse is bold and knows what it is doing. From the lane up on to the bank it can take only one stride, and from there it must put its feet on the bank and jump the post-and-rails with no stride at all. Another obstacle—the bank and ditch—is also easy if the horse has had experience with banks, like the Irish. But, as I know to my cost, banks can cause unpleasant falls. At the first Badminton Three-Day Event, the eventual winner, a fantastically bold and able Thoroughbred called Golden Willow came galloping down to this bank, took off, and cleared the entire bank, with a wide ditch on the landing side, in one leap. Its rider, Capt. John Sheddon must have had a nasty moment in mid-air, when the horse did not touch down on the top of the bank. However, that time he got away with it, and this prodigious leap can go down in history with some of Squire Mytton's feats of over a hundred years ago.

It is this cross-country course above all else that tests the horse's obedience, for with its sharp turns and unusual and difficult fences instant response to the rider's guidance is the deciding factor. It is all the more of a test because of the fact that the horse has already probably covered some twenty miles over roads and tracks, apart from the strenuous steeplechase course, and is bound to be fairly tired by the time it starts the cross-country run. The rider must be in complete sympathy and concord with his mount during this test, and should he feel that it is becoming too tired to tackle a jump at pace, he must give it a breather by taking it quietly over one or two fences. A good rider can save his horse a great deal, but the horse must be initially fit to endure this phase at the necessary pace.

Another hazard during this test is the enthusiasm of the spectators. Naturally, they are only too anxious to see every horse over every fence, and possibly take photographs of them as they jump, but, in their eagerness, they tend to cluster together round the obstacles. It is a habit which could be very dangerous, not only to the competitors but to the spectators themselves. Although the riders are started off at five-minute intervals, it is never possible to gauge exactly when one of them will be riding up to a fence. Some may catch each other up on the way round, or perhaps a horse will drop out or be eliminated, with the result that the gap between competitors might well be as much as fifteen minutes instead of five. Therefore, no one can tell for sure whether a competitor is about to jump a fence or not, and it is most disconcerting for a rider, who is just about to tackle an enormous fence, to find himself suddenly confronted by the startled face of a spectator bobbing up on the other side. Dogs, too, can be a nuisance, for although they are not officially allowed on the course, some people do manage to smuggle them in. These tactics are rather unfair both to the competitors and to the organizers.

After a five-mile cross-country, the horse will naturally be very tired, and so the groom must get it cooled down and relaxed as soon as possible—some horses are a problem to feed after an exciting and strenuous day. The feed must not be too laxative because of the work to be done the following day, but it is a good idea to include glucose in it to build up energy. During the day, the horse's legs will have been under considerable strain and it is therefore advisable to put cooling lotion on them at night. It also keeps the horse warm if its legs are loosely bandaged. When all this has been done, the horse should be left in peace to rest as much as it can before the show jumping on the following day.

Before this jumping begins, the horses are taken out early in the morning to work off any stiffness resulting from their exertions the day before. Each horse is examined by the vet. before being allowed to take part in the third day's test, so there is a double purpose for this early morning ride. When the horse has been passed as sound by the vet., the rider may give it a trial jump before the event to make sure it is supple and obedient.

The jumping course itself is normally quite difficult, not so much from the viewpoint of the height of the obstacles, but from their positions in relation to each other, demanding quick turns and instant obedience from the horses. Although the horses had a hard and strenuous time the day before, they must still submit willingly to the control and guidance of their riders. It is this third phase that proves their ability to jump carefully after galloping over fixed fences across country.

The competitor himself has a part to play other than riding his horse over the jumps. Before the event takes place he must learn and study the course thoroughly, so that when the time comes to enter the arena he has no doubt whatsoever about the positions of the various obstacles. It has happened that a Three-Day Event has been lost on the last day because the rider took the wrong course over the jumps, and surely nothing could be more frustrating after coming through the first two days with flying colours.

On the last day at Badminton, as well as this jumping competition, which also marks the end of the Three-Day Event itself, additional jumping events always take place. Besides a novice competition there is a contest for Grade A horses, which compete for the Badminton Grand Stakes. Prince Hal won this in 1952, then last year, after putting me on the ground during the competition, Tosca made amends for this unladylike behaviour by also winning on the exciting timed jump off. Before the main event of the day, there is always a competition for novices, in which the young horses are able to gain invaluable experience over a well-made course with obstacles under four feet in height of the type they will be meeting later in the bigger competitions. One reason for these additional events on the third day is to ensure a full and interesting programme for the spectators, since, if many of the entrants for the Three-Day Event are eliminated over the first two phases, the last phase would be over very quickly and could not possibly provide a complete day's sport.

To everyone interested in horsemanship at its very best, I can sincerely recommend a visit to Badminton. Not only is it set in the most lovely and picturesque surroundings, but each year the Three-Day Event has been blessed with perfect weather, and that in itself is an attraction with this fickle climate of ours!

No comment!

Chapter Seven

INDOOR AND OUTDOOR ARENAS

HORSEMEN have jumped for sport from time immemorial. Xenophon, the Greek historian, writing twenty-five centuries ago, gives some very accurate instructions on teaching a horse to jump. However, it was not until the turn of this century that the sport began to take its present form, with the development of the forward seat which was first seriously considered by the Italian horseman, Frederico Caprilli. Although military horsemen of the Continent quickly adopted his ideas, the British were more conservative and kept to the old method of sitting back over a fence. As a result, we were left behind in international competitions and it took some time before we were converted to the new methods.

Since the last war, the standard of national show jumping has improved out of all recognition, due to the greater emphasis placed upon international competition and to the increased share taken by civilian riders in the sport. Unfortunately, not all the international shows have been able to keep pace with the great strides made by the sport itself, although of the outdoor arenas our own White City has become recognized throughout the world as the best, both from the point of view of the courses and the excellent organization.

The parade before the Nations Cup in 1948 at White City

The courses there are designed by Colonel M. P. Ansell, chairman of the British Show Jumping Association. The timing of the events is exemplary, in fact you can almost set your watch by the schedule. They are never late and are not allowed to run over time, and there is always something of interest happening in the ring for the spectators to see. Because of this excellent organization and the high standard of the courses, White City provides some of the best show jumping in the world.

Each country has its own typical courses, depending on the person who designs them and the kind of fences available. In the outdoor arena at Madrid, for instance, these are big and a bold horse is needed to jump the large spreads. Great emphasis is placed on jumping at speed, and the Madrid Grand Prix is won by the fastest clear round.

It is one of the few international shows where betting on the jumping is allowed. This tends to slow up the competitions considerably, because each event is divided up into sections of ten or twelve horses and betting takes place on each, as well as the final result. It is necessary, therefore, to wait for each section to finish before that winner can be announced and the bets settled. All this draws out the time taken over competitions, particularly since they may be an hour late starting. The competitors rarely finish before dark and the very short twilight makes it more difficult when one has to jump towards the end of a competition. However, disregard for time is one of Spain's many charms. In fact, it is possibly a reason why, in this modern life of mechanized hurry, people find Spain such an ideal place for a holiday.

Nowadays there is stabling on the show ground, whereas in the past we had our horses about three miles from the ring. The grooms had to ride and lead the horses to the show well before the competitions were due to start, and then they had to stand around in the hot sun awaiting their turn to jump. Today, all this unnecessary discomfort has been eradicated and the facilities are extremely good.

M. Jonquères d'Oriola—winner of the Olympic Gold Medal at Helsinki in 1952, jumping Marquis III in Madrid

The arena itself stands below the town of Madrid on the old front of the Civil War. When we were there in 1951, the countryside round about still showed the scars of war with ruins and large houses riddled with bullet holes. Since then, new stands have been erected and the ground has become a permanent show ground. Looking up at the skyline of the town from the stands, the view is magnificent in the changing light of the evening. Although Madrid is not a large city, it contains the contrast of an old part with its charm and tradition and a new and modern part with the busy rush of present-day life.

The British team went to Lisbon last year for the first time and found the courses excellent, with big fences to jump. The distances between the combinations of fences were often wide so one needed a bold and unhesitant horse to negotiate them. In the six-bar competition, which Prince Hal won, on the final jump-off the last three fences were over six feet with about twelve yards between each. The show was well organized and we were made very comfortable. The horses were stabled by the side of the show ground in delightful surroundings, and we made full use of the pleasant stable yard, after morning exercise, when we sat in the shade of the trees. Our host, the owner of the stables, would bring out bottles of his vintage wine, which we would savour, while talking of our horses and his greyhounds. The show itself was held on the race course, on the ground inside the track. The arena was a lush green with grass that had been specially planted and constantly watered. It certainly made excellent going and was about the only stretch of grass in the district, which consisted mainly of sand.

Original designs and typical gay Portuguese colouring were attractive features of the houses there, most of which were tiled to keep the interiors warm in winter and cool in summer. The tiles gave the outsides a very gay appearance although inside a house they give a rather cooling effect.

One of the most beautiful outdoor arenas in the world is undoubtedly the Piazza di Siena in the Borghesi Gardens in Rome, with the surrounding of picturesque cypresses and umbrella pines. The courses, with the doubles and trebles set at awkward distances, are usually difficult to jump. The Italians specialize, too, in a light type of fence made of birch poles which are difficult to see. Our horses were used to jumping rustic fences in England, but to be really successful in Rome I think one would need a lot of practice over the particular type of courses favoured by the Italians. For instance, one meets two big spreads at such a distance from each other that if the horse puts in two strides between them it will lose the impetus necessary to jump the second one. So it requires a horse of unusual ability to jump right in, take one stride, and then clear the second fence. There is also a big water-jump that is fairly shallow so that the horse does not mind putting his foot in it, thus getting four faults. There is another little water-jump which is called the Bidet and usually has a big fence built over it, or perhaps one in front or behind it. Nevertheless, these difficulties make for a very high standard of jumping at Rome, and the only solution is to practise more at home over varying distances between fences and over water-jumps so that we can overcome the problems.

Famous Italian brothers. Raymondo d'Inzeo on Merano at Ostend. This pair won the *Daily Mail* Champion Cup at White City in 1953. Piero d'Inzeo on Fiano jumping at the Rome Horse Show

The arena itself might well have been a natural Roman arena in the days of Nero, for the spectators sit on tiered terraces and look down on to the riders and horses. The spectators have not always been particularly well disposed towards foreign competitors and the first time our team competed there after the war, they amused themselves by applauding when we knocked a fence. This sometimes makes a rider do a brilliant round in sheer defiance.

My first visit to North Africa was for the jumping at Algiers in 1953. Although the show was held on the race course, as in Lisbon, this time we were jumping on sand. The going was, therefore, extremely deep and it needed a

Major Rook on Starlight

strong and fit horse to stand a chance of success. The courses were solid with big fences. The whole show was looked upon as an elaborate party by the organizers, and we thoroughly enjoyed their hospitality. We were taken to the President's house about a hundred miles inland, through the most breathtaking countryside of lovely hills and orange groves. It was an extraordinary sensation to realize that within an hour's drive from Algiers one could go ski-ing, have a swim in the sea, or ride a camel in the desert.

Last spring I went to Dublin and Cork. I had never jumped at Dublin before, mainly because the Summer Show follows White City and August is a busy time at home. The experience is unique and I was very glad to have the opportunity to go. The Dublin arena is magnificent and I got a great thrill riding over the permanent course with the double and single banks, the stone wall, and deep water-jump. Prince Hal celebrated his first visit by winning a Sweepstake Competition, over fly fences, as opposed to the permanent course.

Last year for the first time an international show was held in Cork. Unfortunately, there were not enough spectators to support it. This was really a great pity, because the organizers went to a lot of trouble to make it a success and ran a first-class show, with the result that the jumping was as good as any ever seen in an international ring. The courses for the competitions were excellent, and the facilities for the horses extremely satisfactory. Tosca celebrated our first appearance in Ireland by winning a very fine bronze shield, the 'An Tostal' trophy, which is now a distinctive decoration by the staircase at Miserden.

People often ask how we manage to combine the sometimes rather hectic social programme with the business of show jumping when we are abroad. It is not always easy. When we are competing in official shows we are usually invited for drinks to each of the embassies in the capital, and since these parties nearly always take place just before the shows, it is difficult to do full justice to the generous hospitality. In any case, there is rarely enough time to talk properly to people at a cocktail party, and never the chance to get to know anyone thoroughly. That is the reason I prefer a dinner or a dance when there is an opportunity to relax and enjoy the stimulating company.

It is very difficult to remember the names of all the people I meet at these parties, too, no matter how determined I am to remember to listen very carefully when I am introduced. It never seems to work out like that when the time comes, and I suddenly realize after a few moments' conversation that I have no idea how to address the person who is talking to me. I think many of us might well try to emulate the Americans in this respect. They always come straight to the point with a 'Meet Miss Smythe', followed by 'Pleased to meet you, *Miss Smythe*', and then, spelling it out, 'Is it S-M-Y-T-H-E —with an *E?*' No doubt then about whom you are talking to! But more often than not they just say, 'Pleased to meet you, Pat', which undoubtedly puts the ensuing conversation on a very firm and friendly basis, but I have never yet been able to decide on the correct procedure for replying to it.

Major Weldon on Kilbarry

Generally speaking, there is not a lot of time for genuine relaxation at these shows. The horses come first, naturally, and much of the time has to be spent working them—rectifying faults before the show, exercising them each morning, and making sure that they are obedient. All this takes even longer when our hotel is some way from the stables, as it very often is.

I wish there were more opportunities to see some of the fine places of the countries we visit —the Louvre in Paris, for instance, or the Prado in Madrid—but to do so means sacrificing the few precious hours left for sleep, and I never seem to get more than about four hours of sleep during these international shows.

Much depends on the climate, too, and the change of food, and although fortunately the conditions rarely have any effect on me, I did catch the Madrid 'tummy bug', with rather disastrous results. Apart from feeling ill and being unable to think of food for two days, at the very moment my name was being called over the microphones for the presentation of the Grand Prix by General Franco, I fainted. When I came to, the microphones were still calling for me, but I was being carted back to the hotel and so I missed the presentation altogether, and the competition that evening.

The international show at Harringay in the autumn is now one of the great indoor shows of the world. As at the White City, good courses and precision timing ensure first-class jumping and continued interest for the spectator. The arena itself, however, is not large and the shortage of space for exercising horses before the competitions is something of a problem. At the moment, there is a cinder patch outside the arena on which to canter them, and there is not much room for many horses to work there at the same time. Even so, it is still possible to supple them up fairly well before jumping, whereas some other international shows make no provision for this work. I have every reason to look forward to the shows at Harringay, because in the past Tosca has won the B.S.J.A. Spurs three times—they were awarded for the highest accumulation of points in National Competitions—and one year Prince Hal and Tosca won the Harringay Spurs, which are awarded for the highest accumulation of points for two horses in International Competitions.

Mlle Jose Bonnand on Charleston

At the first Harringay show it was Finality who won me the B.S.J.A. Spurs—that year the prize was really a pair of spurs, but since then the trophy has been changed to a most useful bridle.

The spectators at Harringay are always very enthusiastic and the interest has grown considerably during the last few years. One of the reasons may be the exciting competitions that have been shown on television. Over eight thousand people can be accommodated and the performances are booked up many months in advance.

The Paris show has an arena the same size as Harringay, yet it can seat fifteen thousand, and the spectators are so keen that they pay up to three pounds for a seat. Good prize money is put up and the trophies themselves are very attractive, with such prizes as cigarette boxes and clocks instead of the usual cups. When Hal won the Grand Prix there last year the course was big but did not present the rider with many problems. However, most of the other events were speed competitions and at times we were galloping over fences higher than five foot. A horse had to be very bold and handy when tackling these obstacles at speed.

It was difficult to know exactly when to prepare the horses for a competition, as half the horses in each competition were brought into a little inner collecting ring at the same time. There they waited until they jumped their round. If one wanted to work the horses this had to be done in the morning, for the show beginning at eight in the evening, for the only place to warm them up before competing was a passage-way behind the stadium. It was impossible to do much there, such as turn or circle, because it was far too narrow. There were always so many other horses galloping up and down that it was hard to find a place in the queue, without exciting one's horse. The reason for the lack of space is that the stadium is in the centre of Paris, and there is nowhere to lay down a circular ring for preliminary exercise.

There was more space outside the arena at Marseilles, and the big jumping arena enables

Harringay Arena in 1949

William Steinkraus on Democrat, a winner at Madison Square Garden, New York

the horses to settle down more quickly when they once start to jump. Prince Hal excelled himself by jumping for the three nights without touching a fence—eleven rounds in all. The people there were charming and extremely hospitable, and we thoroughly enjoyed our tour of the 'sights' which included a boat trip round the Old Port.

The Swiss show at Zurich was one of the few where all the teams were put up at the same hotel, and this was a most pleasing feature. Normally we are segregated from the foreign teams and never have a chance to meet and talk with them at length. It was most refreshing to be able to meet one's rivals on a social rather than a competitive basis for a change.

One of the problems at this show was the surface of the stadium, which was a converted ice rink. The ice was covered with some sort of matting and peat spread on top, so that if the horses put their feet through the layer of peat on to a join in the matting beneath they were inclined to slip. But it was a vast arena for an indoor show, big enough, in fact, to have a bank at one end. Geneva is now the only venue for an international indoor show in Switzerland.

The two international shows in the United States are at New York and Harrisburg, Pennsylvania, and except for the Thousand-Dollar Stakes no prize money is awarded. The jumping at Harrisburg is incorporated into a National Farm Show, at which every type of American horse can be seen—trotters, hackneys, pacing horses, Tennessee Walking Horses, and the three- and five-gaited horses. On the whole the jumping courses at Harrisburg needed more original planning and better fences.

From here the horses were taken to New York by road in enormous articulated trucks, which were driven at over 70 miles an hour with six horses in each. The roads were so good, however, that they had a very smooth journey and were none the worse for being driven at such great, and unusual, speeds.

One very sad incident marred the journey. The truck in front of ours caught fire and two very valuable hackneys in it were burnt to death before they could be released. Being an articulated vehicle the driver did not realize what had happened until it was too late.

The stabling and general facilities at New York were the most difficult that we have encountered. The only available stabling space was beneath Madison Square Garden where there was little drainage, with the result that the atmosphere became very stuffy. There was nowhere to muck out the horses, so that they were standing all the time on dirty bedding.

There was nowhere to exercise them. If one took them out of the building one found oneself on Eighth Avenue riding in and out of the rushing traffic. Needless to say, no one ventured forth. The only alternative was to exercise early in the morning in the arena itself with all the other horses, and since the arena was smaller even than at Harringay the confusion can be imagined.

It was not surprising, then, that the jumping suffered—a horse which has not even had a preliminary trot can hardly be expected to jump a clear round—and the standard of jumping was consequently lowered. Again the problem was the lack of available space, but if a place could be found for one ring to be laid down, so that the horses could canter before the competition, better jumping would be the result.

The courses themselves consisted of difficult doubles and trebles, and a number of thin fences. Horses are not impressed by these light, high obstacles. Their attention is taken by the solid bases which distract them from the thin bar at the top. The distance from Europe with the competition of their international teams has prevented the American shows from getting their courses up to present-day standards.

However, they certainly gave the teams their generous hospitality. At our hotel, the Waldorf, a room was set aside every night where free drinks were served and we could meet and talk with the other competitors. That was only one of the ways in which they welcomed us to their country.

The Canadian show at Toronto was exceedingly well organized, and was part of a fat stock show, as at Harrisburg. The stables were ample and airy, and a small arena was available for exercising the horses. The main arena was large but unfortunately the courses were not very interesting, mainly owing to the fact that one had to jump up one side, down the other, and then back up the middle again. With a little more ingenuity in design, this could have been a really first-class show. As it was, the standard of jumping was not high. It was greatly enlivened, however, by the many activities going on all round the stadium. Square dancing competitions were being held in various parts of the building, while the fruit, vegetable, and flower shows were a delightful spectacle.

Although the rider and horse receive all the applause and glamour in the glare of the show ring, there would be neither glamour nor applause for either of them if it were not for the efficiency of the organization which carries on calm and unperturbed behind the scenes. This

The presentation of the teams at Madison Square in 1953

Royal Agricultural Winter Fair, Toronto. The ring is set up for the Jumping Class, with committee members on telephones to do scoring

is particularly true when we are travelling abroad, without the luxury of the American's articulated transport. And this is where Pauline comes in. It is her tireless, unseen efforts that keep my horses fit to compete. For she sees that the horses are in the right place at the right time, ready for jumping. Apart from keeping them in top condition during long journeys and strenuous shows.

This is not always an easy assignment. The railway wagons in which the horses travel hold either two or four horses, and she always travels in the wagon with them. Unlike horse boxes, which are not practicable when travelling abroad, these wagons have neither padding on the walls nor partitions to divide them into separate quarters. Pauline usually manages to contrive an arrangement of poles and ropes at each end to give each horse a separate 'compartment', while she settles down with her belongings in the middle. And the wagons are not always very clean. Their use is not devoted solely to conveying horses and their grooms. On their last journey they might have been carrying chalk and their interiors still thick with white dust. Or it might have been butter, or even cheese.

Pauline never leaves the horses on their own during a train journey, because some sudden disturbance might upset or frighten them. She always carries a torch with her, too, and if, during the hours of darkness, they need assurance she flashes it quickly, and when they realize she is there they at once become calm and settle down again.

Sometimes the journeys last as long as five days and, although there are frequent lengthy halts, it is never possible to exercise the horses. The entrance to the wagon is very much higher than the station platform, so without ramps the horses cannot be unloaded, and ramps are not provided. Originally, the horses are loaded into the wagon from a specially raised platform and ramps are not therefore necessary.

There is a fine spirit of comradeship and goodwill between the girls who travel with the horses, and they are always prepared to help each other out over personal difficulties. When one of the girls lost her passport travelling from Portugal to Madrid, it was mainly through the concerted efforts of the others that she ever reached the show at all.

The customs officials at the border refused to

let her through, and at one time it seemed as if they would also refuse entrance to the rest of the British horses. So the girls put all their money together and telephoned the British Embassy at Lisbon. They had just about enough for the call. The girl who had lost her passport was ordered to return to Lisbon, where she was told she would have to stay for three days to qualify for a permit to cross the border. The customs were ordered to let the others through. The girl could not speak a word of the language but she had to travel to Lisbon alone. She eventually arrived at Madrid six days later on the day of the show itself, the President of the Lisbon show himself having very kindly given her a lift in his car. Meanwhile, the other girls had been looking after her horses for her, an additional work in which they all helped.

I well remember an experience I once had with our own customs officials. It was in 1949 when I went with the British team to France, Belgium, and Switzerland.

Leona, my little grey mare, won a prize in the last competition at Geneva the day before we returned home. It was a lovely clock mounted in a stirrup iron, with little silver horseshoes on the hands, and I was worried that the customs officers might confiscate it because I was certainly not in a position to pay a large duty.

As we neared our coast, I began to wonder whether to declare it or leave it wrapped up inside my riding coat. But honesty prevailed, and when we reached the customs office I took it out of my case, together with a silver compact with 'Coupe Kestos' engraved on it, and a light tin cup set into a heavy marble base, which were other prizes I had won.

Anxiously I began a long explanation to the officer, but, with a wave of his hand, he cut me short.

'That's all right,' he said with a smile. 'You can bring in as many of these as you like. We can do with them.'

It was my twenty-first birthday.

The Wembley Arena during the Grand Prix des Nations of the Olympic Games in 1948

Prince Hal winning the Puissance, Paris, November 1954. At both shows he also won the Grand Prix

Prince Hal winning the Algiers Grand Prix, 1955

Chapter Eight

TOSCA AND HAL AT HOME

PRINCE HAL came to Miserden one wet and windy Saturday morning in April 1950. Nobody thought that this excitable red-haired former race-horse would eventually become a top-class show jumper—and least of all, I am sure, did he!

It was the morning of the Cotswold Hunt point-to-point, and as Hal was being unloaded and introduced to his new box, I was busy loading Only Just, my ride for the Ladies Race that afternoon, into our ancient cattle lorry. The thought occurred to me that it might be more appropriate to substitute Prince Hal in the new race-horse box for Only Just and the old green lorry. But we left him to settle into his new home, and as he stood thoughtfully contemplating his fresh surroundings we set off for the point-to-point.

That evening when we returned to Miserden, Only Just received all the honour and attention, for he had run a great race in the afternoon, so I only had time to introduce myself to Prince Hal once again and make sure he had settled down.

The next day I took him out for a ride. An hour later I was in despair and we were both in a lather. Perhaps they were right after all, I kept on telling myself—all those people who insisted he was not the right material to make a show jumper. Perhaps they were right and I had made a terrible mistake. But I could not afford mistakes like that, not when they cost £150, which was the price I had paid for Hal.

Although he had many of the qualities necessary for a show jumper, with athletic ability and an obvious love of jumping, he was hot and excitable when he should have been calm and unflustered. He was apt to lose his temper and forget his mouth, leaving me with no control over him. The slightest sound was a nervous distraction and reminded him of the noisy race-course which had formerly been his accustomed surroundings, and he could not understand why now he was not allowed to gallop.

He was extremely one-sided and unable to turn in one direction. In fact, his backbone would bend only one way and when I tried to turn him the other way, he flatly refused to co-operate. He was suddenly finding life very tiresome and was, I am sure, longing to be back on the race-course with the cheering crowds and tense excitement. But he soon began to understand that I had other plans in store for him, and gradually started to enjoy his new way of living.

Even today he sometimes loses his temper when I am working him and making him do something he does not particularly want to do. He dislikes moving sideways because of his sensitivity to leg pressure, and I often imagine him saying to himself: 'I really can't bear this any longer. Does she think my patience is unlimited?'

When he is in hard work, Hal always likes to go to bed after breakfast. After his morning feed at about seven-thirty, he will lie down for a couple of hours and have a quiet rest. Often when we want to get him up for early work he refuses to be disturbed, and when we came back from Paris and Brussels last year he was so tired after the journey he even refused to get up for breakfast! So he had it in bed—on the floor.

I do not mind at all how much he lies down, because the more rest a show jumper gets in this way the better it is for his legs and tendons.

Schooling Prince Hal at home

Unfortunately some jumpers are inclined to get stiff and are afraid that if they do lie down they will not be able to get up again. They will even sit on their mangers to rest instead of lying down.

One of the dangers in a stable is for a horse to become cast, which is to say that while rolling in his box he gets wedged against the wall with his legs folded up. When this happens there is not sufficient room between the horse and the wall for him to be able to get to his feet again, and in his struggles to stand up he might very well strain a muscle or even panic and exhaust himself.

Prince Hal often gets cast on the first day of an international show when he rolls in a box which is unfamiliar to him. Then the only thing to do is to turn him back on the other side, so that his legs are free and away from the wall, and he can scramble to his feet again. He now wears a special roller, with a high piece in the middle of his back. This is supposed to prevent a horse from rolling right over.

After breakfast he is groomed and made ready for the morning work. Occasionally, if he feels that we have interrupted his after-breakfast snooze too soon, he lies down again after his grooming and we have to begin all over again. It is a most disconcerting habit! Most horses when they leave the stables in the morning are fresh and lively, but gradually calm down during their work. Hal, on the other hand, comes out of the stable rather tired and listless, and the more work he does the more excited and naughty he gets. At the end of it he goes back to the stable just as if he were a young race-horse about to begin his exercise

This daily work consists of obedience training, cantering and stopping, changing pace and generally making the horses supple. It is most important that they should be supple, like an athlete, and bend the way you want them to from head to tail. When jumping in small arenas they become inclined to anticipate the turns and tend to cut corners. This makes it very difficult to approach an obstacle straight. Immediately they get the indication that you are about to turn they will cut the corner without looking at the next fence soon enough. The aim is to train them to turn with their head first so that they can see the next fence. Then there is more time to judge the obstacle. A horse in its natural state, galloping round a field, will always turn with its shoulder first and its head bent away from the direction in which it is turning, therefore it must be trained by the rider to make it bend inwards when turning. For international jumping it is most important to make the horse obedient for quick turns and to obey the rider's leg instantaneously.

I do not always work the horses on these obedience tests. A lot depends on the state of the ground and whether I feel they might have become rather tired with jumping after a long period of shows. Then I take them out for a cross-country ride to cheer them up, and I know that they enjoy every minute of it and come back to routine work with renewed zest.

When their work is over they are always walked back to the stables to let them cool down. If they are still hot, they are rubbed down and perhaps walked around in the sunshine for a while, wearing only a head collar. We let them pick some grass to help them to relax, but they are never allowed any water until they are completely cool. It is important to see that their ears are warm, because they act as a kind of barometer which shows how they feel themselves. If their ears are cold, then you know that the horse is cold too. They have their mid-day feed when they have cooled down and usually rest in the afternoon.

Out of the jumping season, if the weather is suitable, they go out for two hours each day to play in a field. They love this period of complete freedom and spend most of the time cantering and galloping round, with an occasional break to eat the grass. We never turn Prince Hal and Tosca out in the same field together. They are both horses of strong character and great energy, and would excite each other too much. So we send out a pony with each one in turn and it stands calm and unruffled eating away in the middle of the field, refusing to be disturbed by the antics of either Hal or Tosca. As a result, the horse comes back to stand beside the pony between his bursts of energy, and in this way the pony acts as a tether in the middle of the field and ensures that the horse does not become too excited and hurt itself on the fence. This is

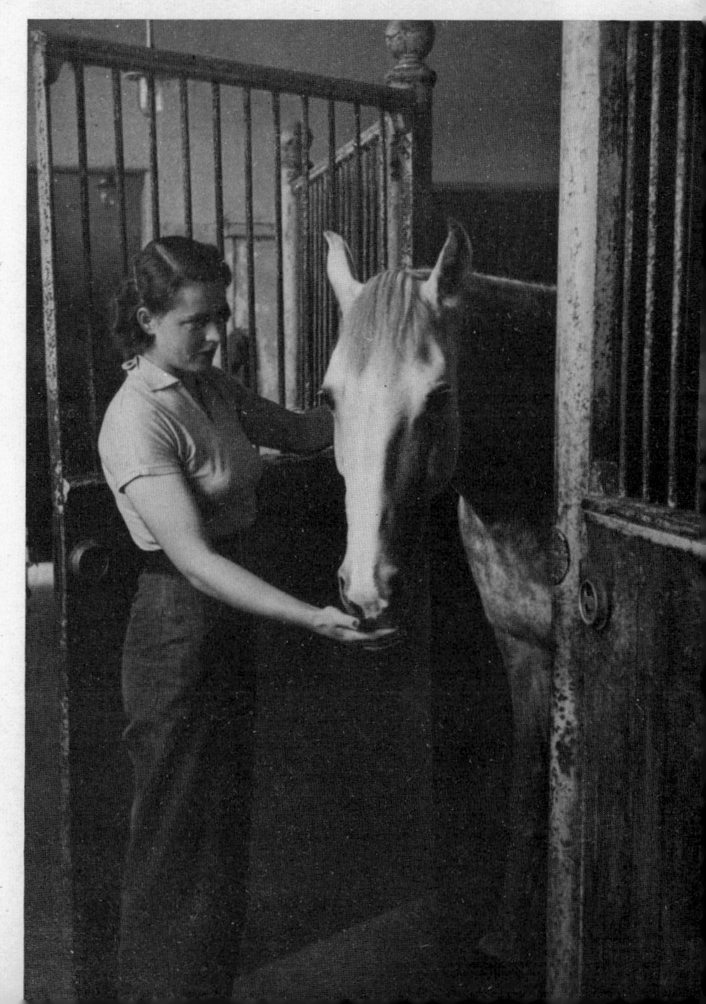

Tosca in the stables at Miserden

Flanagan and Prince Hal

also the reason that a donkey is often put in a field with young Thoroughbreds. Some horses like Prince Hal are merely like mischievous schoolboys. Hal loves to nip off a button from your jacket, or gently remove your gloves or hat. Sometimes when he nips a bit too hard, and contacts flesh, he looks very guilty. At one time he always found the blacksmith's braces an irresistible attraction. As the smith was bending down over his front shoes, he caught the braces carefully between his teeth and, stretching the elastic to its limit, suddenly let go. As the blacksmith jumped up in surprise, Hal, with an innocent twinkle in his eye, turned the other way with supreme unconcern as if it were nothing at all to do with him.

Tosca, on the other hand, is far less impish and a pair more dissimilar than she and Prince Hal would be hard to find. The more solid of the two, she needs work to keep her supple. She must have small fences to jump when being schooled to build up her confidence, and she hates touching a fence. Being so small, she must be fresh if she is to give of her best, but she must also be sufficiently obedient to accept help from her rider.

When she came to Miserden, six months after the arrival of Hal, Tosca was very wild and in poor condition. I suspect that she had not been treated too well at some time, and consequently a resentment of human beings had grown within her.

A horse which has been misused or roughly handled reacts in one of two ways. If it has a strong character, it grows to hate humans and quickly learns to retaliate to rough treatment with a particular brand of its own. But if its character is weak, it merely becomes cowed and frightened. The moment you enter the box, you can tell if the horse trusts you or if it is on the defensive.

Tosca's strong character was the reason for

Arthur Roseblade shoeing Leona at Miserden forge

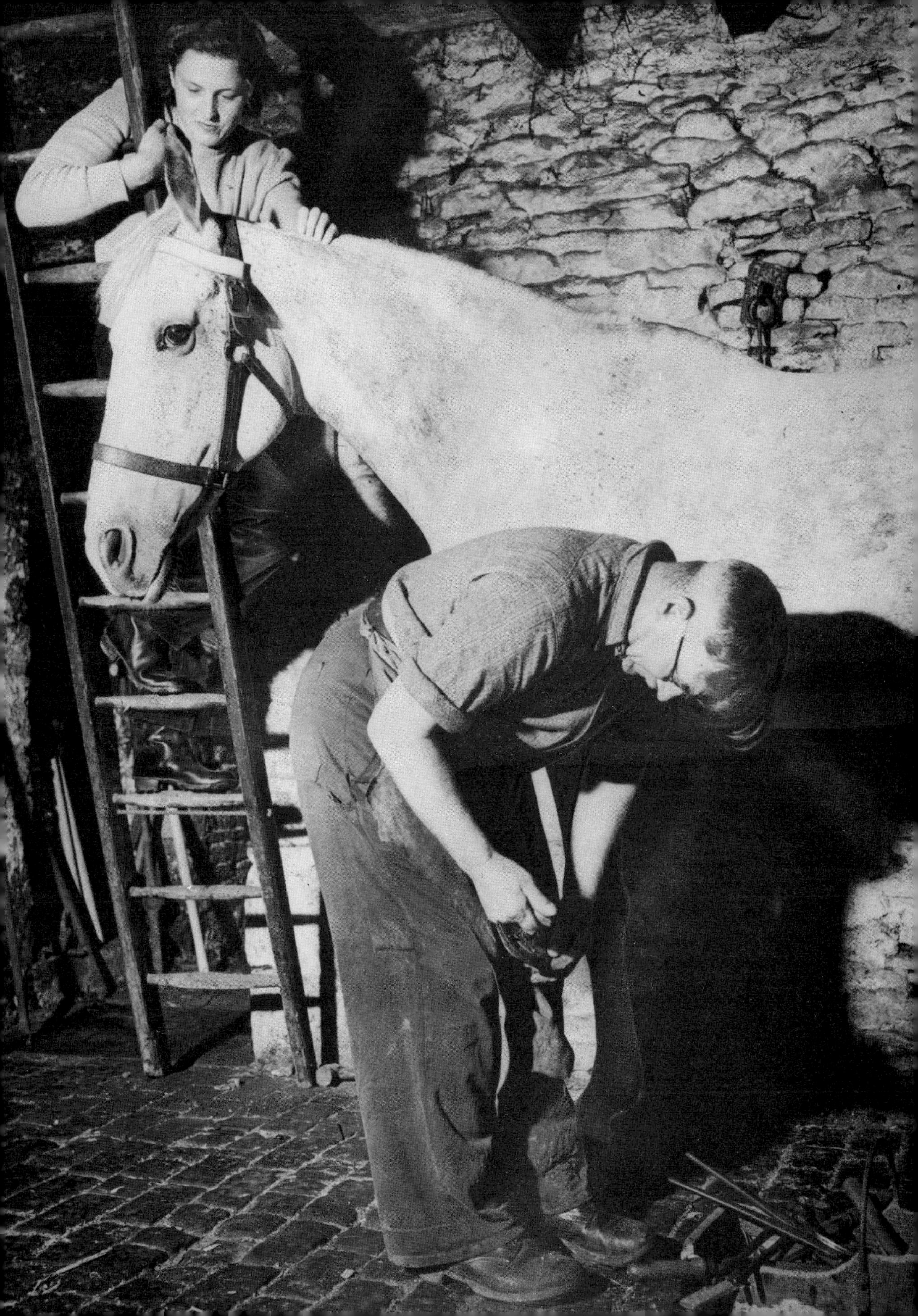

Miserden House

her resentment and dislike of people, and one had to be very careful when mucking out her box. A sudden noise or quick movement would immediately put her on the defensive, and she would swing round so that her quarters were against you. I was once trapped for a quarter of an hour in her box in this way.

Something I did must have startled her because in a second she had me pinned in a corner of the box. I could see that she had no intention of letting me get away, either. I was afraid to touch her quarters or to shout to anyone outside in the yard in case she became more frightened and kicked me. Therefore, I talked to her quietly and then pretended I had something in my pocket. Eventually she turned her head to see what it was and I was able to catch hold of her. I went on talking to her for a time to show that I was her friend and also to explain to her that I did not enjoy being threatened with her hind hooves.

It took about six months to rid her of this distrustful attitude, and even then it would spring up again if she were mildly corrected for some disobedience. But today nothing worries her and she could not be more friendly towards everyone.

Although I had ridden Tosca when I had tried her out before buying her, it was not until she arrived at Miserden that I was able to find out what she could really do. I soon found that she could do a lot of things, but not many of the things she did showed the qualities which indicated she would make a show jumper. I

Friends taking two of the horses out to grass

will never forget that first ride after she arrived at Miserden.

Mother came out with me on another horse to lead the way. We came to a small broken-down wall and she went over first. Following behind, Tosca leapt over in a huge bound and immediately ran away on the other side, racing three times round the field while I tried despairingly to stop her. When I did manage to pull her up she at once started flybucking. Eventually I managed to control her and, going across the field, we came to another wall slightly higher than the first. This was the only place we could jump and again Mother went first. Tosca flybucked up to the jump, so that I had no control over her whatsoever. At the last moment she stopped, and refused to jump. Then she seemed to go completely crazy and flybucked round the field.

I began to wonder if I had really made a mistake this time. Tosca was obviously far too excitable for a show jumper, whose main requisite is its ability to respond to control. But I hate having to admit defeat. For one thing it is very bad for the horse's character, and for another, it can often be costly financially. This would certainly have been the case with Tosca for whom, like Prince Hal, I had paid £150—a bargain price admittedly, but a sum I could not afford to throw away.

It was obvious that first day that Tosca was not going to jump that particular wall. She was so uncontrollable that I decided to train her on the flat for several weeks and not even look

Schooling Mr. Hanson's Flanagan at Miserden

at a jump until I had more control over her. Like most horses she preferred to go one way, in her case to the left, so I worked her to the right. The majority of horses do have a tendency towards turning to the left, because when they are young they are usually led from this side. Also, they are bridled and saddled from the near side and usually lunged to the left, so they develop the habit of moving round in a left-handed circle. It is important, therefore, that a young horse should be made to understand that there are two sides to the question and, although it may be incorrect, it should be saddled and mounted from the off side as well.

Today, Tosca loves her jumping. When she walks down to the field for her work, she looks at all the fences eagerly as we pass them, and I can imagine her thinking: 'There's a place we could jump. Are we going to jump that one?' When she has done well at a show she arches her neck and sometimes gives a little buck after jumping a clear round. Then she looks round at me for her reward, a piece of apple or carrot, or perhaps a tuft of grass, but rarely a lump of sugar because after a strenuous round a horse prefers something juicy to quench its thirst.

Almost every horse likes winning a rosette. Tosca is no exception and she loves to show off to the crowd as she canters round the ring with a rosette fluttering on her bridle. I have had horses that have nearly bucked me off after they have won, whether from the sheer joy of winning or because of a wicked sense of humour I have never been able to decide. But it would certainly be humiliating for a rider to fall off while receiving a rosette, after successfully negotiating a course of difficult fences.

After an uncertain beginning, Tosca lost no

Prince Hal, Windy, and Bliss at the entrance of the stables

time in settling down and becoming a star of her sport. Her first important show was Harringay, in the autumn of 1951, where she won the B.S.J.A. Spurs and two other events. The next year, her first full season's jumping, she was the Leading Horse of Great Britain. In 1953, although she missed the early part of the season through laming herself abroad, she was again the Leading Jumper by the end of the season.

I am grateful to Prince Hal and Tosca for many things, but particularly for the opportunity they have given me of experiencing the enjoyment and thrills of show jumping. It is a most absorbing and fascinating sport, and its popularity is steadily growing as our teams bring back more prizes from abroad.

It is a sport which teaches one that there are more important things in life than one's own little whims and fancies. Above all it teaches self-control, that characteristic so essential for dealing with animals when sudden loss of temper can ruin weeks of training, and undo the many hours of patient work to achieve harmony and confidence in the partnership of horse and rider.

It is only through this working partnership that a lasting friendship can be built up with the animal, and there are many stories of horses showing that they remember people who were their friends, perhaps after years of separation. My first show jumper, Finality, always remembered me although I only saw her at yearly intervals after she had been sold; and Prince Hal and Tosca can pick me out in a crowd although I may not be dressed in riding clothes.

Of course, they may only be thinking: 'There's Pat. I wonder if this means more hard work?' But the recognition is a good reward.

Chapter Nine

A VISIT TO THE ROYAL MEWS

It has often been said that no people in the world can put on such a lavish and colourful display as the British. The Coronation was proof that this is true. We seem to have that ability for meticulous organization and timing which no other country possesses. And it is certainly true that no one loves a procession more dearly than ourselves. The pageantry, the waving of the flags and banners, the rousing strains of brass bands, and the dazzling colours of the uniforms, all combine to stir us deeply. And with a royal procession there is no limit to our feeling of pride and enjoyment.

But few of us are lucky enough to be able to take a glimpse behind the scenes at the Royal Mews and see the actual preparations for our processions. What we see as one of the crowd is the finished article, the outcome of supreme organization which started many weeks before the chosen day of the procession. Yet it is possible for anyone to visit the Royal Mews and see something of the everyday life of the people who live there. It is merely a question of applying for permission, and every Wednesday afternoon there is an endless stream of visitors being shown round by top-hatted grooms, gatekeepers, and postillions: school children, townswomen's guilds, women's institutes, foreign tourists, provincial visitors, and even film stars from overseas—all these make up the various parties which have applied for, and obtained, permission to tour the Royal Mews. And it is a fascinating experience.

In that quiet square to the south of Buckingham Palace are the many buildings which go to make up this home of royal pomp and ceremony: stables, coach houses, harness rooms, forge, and living accommodation for the fifty families of chauffeurs, postillions, grooms, gate porters, and carriage washers. It is an entirely self-contained unit, a 'family' working together in complete unison and harmony.

For a visitor to the Mews, the coach houses on the east side of the square are probably the main attraction, for there the three majestic carriages of almost fairy-book appearance are kept—the Gold State Coach, the Irish State Coach, and the Glass Coach.

My own first impression of the Gold State Coach was its immense size, 24 feet long, over 13 feet high, and weighing 4 tons. It is the only coach fitted with a brake, and this must be a very necessary precaution, with this great weight coming downhill behind the horses. It was designed by Sir William Chambers and, under his supervision, was finished in 1761. The delicate paintings on the doors and panels by the Italian artist Cipriani can really be appreciated, and the beautiful gilt carvings are even more magnificent when seen at close quarters. These carvings are all cleaned with soap and water, using a very soft camel hair brush, and it must take hours of work to cover such a vast area.

The Duke of Portland told a fascinating story a few months ago about a dream his father had just before the Coronation of King Edward VII. He dreamt that, owing to the height of the crown on top, the coach got stuck under Horse Guards Arch during the Coronation procession. Panic and pandemonium broke out, with the horses rearing and

The State Coach with the Windsor Greys

plunging and the large crowd scattering frantically in all directions.

The dream had been so realistic that the next morning he asked his commanding officer's permission to measure the arch. The whole thing was ridiculed at first but eventually permission was granted. He measured the height of the crown and then the arch. It *was* too low to take the State Coach. Later it was found that during Queen Victoria's long reign the road had been raised by continual repairs, and there was no longer room for the coach to pass beneath the arch.

I was intrigued by the fluorescent lighting installed in most of the coaches. At first, this modern innovation seemed slightly out of place amongst such old pageantry and tradition. But there is a very good reason for it. Without it, one would not be able to see the occupants on a dull or dreary day, and since it is also tinted pink it gives the impression of sunshine inside the coaches.

Today, the Gold State Coach is used only for royal processions, when it is drawn by the famous eight Windsor Greys.

In another building I saw the Irish State Coach, bought by Queen Victoria from the Lord Mayor of Dublin, who was also a coachmaker. In the later part of her reign, the Queen used it for all State occasions, and after the death of Albert, the Prince Consort, she never rode again in the Gold State Coach. The Irish Coach is deep blue and gold, superbly sprung, and is used by the sovereign for the Opening of Parliament, levees and funerals. It is usually drawn by four horses and the gilt lacing round the top of the coach shows the emblems of Great Britain with the Tudor Rose, Thistle, and Shamrock. For the Coronation drive in 1953 it was used by the Queen Mother.

The Irish State Coach

The last of the trio, the Glass Coach, is the one used by Princess Elizabeth and Prince Philip for their drive through London after their wedding ceremony. As a result, it has become known as the bridal coach to the occupants of the Mews.

In addition to these three glittering coaches, there are six State landaus; a State road landau, which was the favourite of King Edward VII, and now used when visiting foreign royalty are met at Victoria Station; five semi-State landaus; nine 'Clarences' used at the Coronation by the Prime Minister's procession; five broughams; and two barouches. All these carriages are beautifully sprung and can travel over the roughest of roads without discomfort to their passengers. Owing to the increase in the number of cars, a few of the older carriages were sold some years ago to a film company. But the old horses are never sold when their active days are over. They are 'pensioned off' and put out to grass for the rest of their lives.

The first thing I saw when we went into the ante-room, which leads into the coach house where the State Coach is kept, were the Prince of Wales's feathers up on the wall. These had particular significance for me because my first pony had been bred on the Prince of Wales's estate at Tor Royal, and Pixie had been branded with the feathers. Fascinating, too, was the little coach made for Prince Charles by some Australian school teachers, and the prints of the State liveries worn by the postillions, grooms, head coachman, and outriders which hung on the wall. There was even a print of the Royal sleigh. An important comfort for the past generations was still on show, the footwarmer used by royalty during State processions.

When we went into the stables I was at once impressed by their immaculate condition, with the plaited straw down the side of each stall and the clean brick passage down the centre, finely sprinkled with sand to prevent the horses slipping.

The horses, too, looked extremely well and are kept perfectly, with one groom looking

State Landau

after two horses. They are all very big, standing over 16·2 hands up to 17·2 hands. Amongst the carriage horses are some very fine Cleveland Bays which have strength combined with the quality for their work.

As we walked across the courtyard towards the saddle-rooms, a coach drove in. It had just taken the Ambassador of Panama, Margot Fonteyn's husband, to the Palace to present his credentials to the Queen. The two bay horses pulling the coach looked very fit and after trotting back they were still quite dry.

In the first saddle-room, I was immediately attracted by the red morocco leather Coronation harness, with its richly gilt coats of arms, and the little figures of St. George and the Dragon adorning it. It is a most beautiful set of harness. We also saw some of the black harness used for other processions. One man spends all his time cleaning the harness here, for as soon as he has finished down one side of the room he has to begin again with the other. So his work is never done.

The royal saddles are kept in the other room. One of the side saddles used by Queen Alexandra is unique with its one pommel on the off side, instead of the usual two on the near side. We were shown the saddle used by Queen Victoria, with her own saddle cloth and her whips, and a very typical Mexican saddle presented to the Prince of Wales. The horn was decorated with the figure of a man riding a bucking bull.

Opposite the numerous saddles on the other side of the room were the racing colours worn by Ivor Anthony, when he won the Grand National on Ambush II in 1900, the horse owned by the Prince of Wales, who was later to become King Edward VII. These colours have only recently been presented to the Royal Mews.

From here we walked over to the large indoor riding school where the horses are exercised in bad weather and where, before a procession, the Queen may ride Winston to get the feel of him again. The school is also

State Coach Postillions

used for training the horses to the sights and sounds of a big London procession, with the flag waving and music, as they do at the Police Horse Training Centre at Imber Court. Incidentally, these police horses are often permitted to work in the Royal Mews indoor school, where they get a chance to canter and work at faster paces, as a much needed contrast to their ordinary work outside in the streets where they can only walk and trot.

Most people like to speculate on the great cost of a royal procession, particularly when they see the brightly coloured liveries of the coachmen, grooms, postillions, out-riders, and footmen. However, not one new livery had to be bought for the Queen's Coronation two years ago.

This was just as well when one realizes the formidable cost of a new uniform, with its expensive cloth and yards of braid and fine gold thread which has to be worked entirely by hand. I have no idea of the exact cost of a new livery today, but at the time of the Coronation of King George VI, way back in the thirties, it was almost £150. Today, it is probably three times as much.

An unwritten rule of the Mews is that a postillion must not be over 5 feet 7 inches. In this way, uniforms can be handed down from man to man, repaired, altered, and refurbished as and when necessary. Needless to say, the greatest possible care is taken of the liveries, and when they are not in use they are always wrapped carefully away.

Recruits to the Mews staff have usually had some past experience with horses, for despite the greatly increased number of cars now garaged there, the main daily activity is still with the horses. However, a man without experience but with a genuine love for horses might also be employed, providing he was conscientious, patient, and could adapt himself to the split-second timing and organization necessary for royal processions.

The practical day-to-day organization is in the hands of the Superintendent, who is responsible for running the Mews community and its royal horses. Everything that happens comes under his jurisdiction, from a short car ride to a Coronation itself.

At the supreme head of the Department is the Master of the Horse, the Duke of Beaufort. He is officially responsible for the horses, carriages, coachmen, postillions, and chauffeurs. This responsibility is handed on to an officer known as the Crown Equerry, who arranges the processions and supervises the transport. But the man on the spot is the Superintendent. He is in charge of the daily activities of horses and staff.

One of his many duties is to note in the official record book the movements of every horse, car, or carriage when it leaves the Mews on official duty. At the same time, the nature of the duty must be recorded. This book has been kept now for hundreds of years and some of the entries for years gone by must make fascinating reading. It is also his job to supervise the harness and equipment, watch over the health of the horses, arrange for the purchase of new ones, the retirement of the old ones no longer fit for royal service, and the training of the young horses.

Every carriage which leaves the Mews is not necessarily going out on a procession. For instance, there is the deep blue brougham of the Queen's Messenger drawn by a single bay horse, with its top-hatted coachman, which moves continually between the Palace and Whitehall with the Queen's despatches.

There are the ambassadors who go to the Palace to present their credentials to the Queen. Whenever a new envoy is appointed to the Court of St. James, enough carriages for the needs of his establishment are despatched to the embassy to bring the ambassador and his senior diplomats to Court. In addition, of course, there are the 'official' occasions such as Trooping the Colour, State drives, presentations, weddings, visits of foreign royalty, and State Openings of Parliament.

In one corner of the Mews square is the room where the people who live there hold their dances, concerts, and whist drives. Hanging on one wall is the picture of an old mare, Brownie, which was ridden by King George V for Trooping the Colour ceremonies.

It was always said by the Mews inhabitants that this intelligent little mare knew just as much about the ceremony as the Equerry or the Superintendent. On more than one occasion she walked calmly up to the King's place on Horse Guards' Parade, turned herself round without the King even having to touch the reins, and faced the assembly as if she had been carrying out the same manœuvre every day of her life.

Stories are still told in the Mews of King George V's keenness for punctuality. If he were going riding in Hyde Park in the morning, the horses would never be ordered for 8 o'clock, or even 8.30. It was perhaps 8.4 or 8.23, or some equally peculiar time. And he would always be there exactly to the minute.

It was not until 1830 that the Royal Mews came to Buckingham Palace. Before that it was situated on the north side of Charing Cross where Trafalgar Square is today. At that time, it was known as the Royal Mewse, the place where the king's falcons were 'mewed'. During the reign of Henry VIII, after a fire at the Lomesbury Royal Stables, the horses joined the falcons at Charing Cross. They stayed there until the middle of the nineteenth century, and when Pall Mall road was built they were moved to Buckingham Palace.

Chapter Ten

POINT-TO-POINTS

ONE of the greatest thrills in riding is racing in point-to-points. This is strictly an amateur sport and no professional jockey is allowed to compete. Even horses that have won steeplechases under National Hunt Rules are barred from certain races, although they are sometimes allowed to enter for the open events. Each Hunt has its own point-to-point and today the standard of riding and the class of the horses is extremely high. In fact, a horse can progress from point-to-points to achieving the great distinction of winning the Gold Cup at Cheltenham, such as Four Ten, the 1954 winner. My own point-to-point horses may not have been quite so ambitious as this, yet I can still recall the great thrill of winning my first Ladies' Race on Only Just in 1949.

Only Just was owned and bred by a friend who lived nearby. The year before, he had shown me this minute little animal, saying that, if I cared to train and prepare him for point-to-point racing, he was sure he would give me my first win. At the same time, he told me something about the horse and how he had got his name.

His mother, Just Jane, who had been a great point-to-point winner, had died at his birth and at one time it was touch and go whether the colt himself would live. It was certainly a very near thing and he 'only just' survived. Added to this handicap, Only Just was brought up during the war so he never grew very big or strong. However, being naturally very quick and light on his feet, he was a charming little horse to ride and loved his jumping, either racing or hunting. His greatest drawback was his tendency to think too much. When he came back from hunting, he would imagine all the exciting things he had done or seen during the day, and would sweat all night and forget to eat his supper. If he thought he might be going racing, he stood trembling with excitement in his box. We devised all kinds of methods so that he would not realize in advance that he was going to race, such as leaving his mane unplaited until we arrived at the race-course, but somehow he always seemed to know.

My first point-to-point race had been with the Ledbury Hunt at Bushey Park, near Tewkesbury. The horse I rode was a grand bay called Dandy Dick, and owned by my uncle, Colonel Gordon Smythe. A year later I was to win over the same course on Only Just. It was only his second race, having previously come in fourth at the Cotswold Vale point-to-point, so we were naturally both tensed and excited.

There was a very good field for our race that day with two joint favourites, one of which was My Man, who had won the race the year before. Only Just was one of the outsiders at 12 to 1, a very long price for a point-to-point. As we waited at the start I thought back to that race a year ago, remembering how the big, strong Dandy Dick had galloped fresh and excited down the slope towards the first fence, and hit it with a resounding crash right down at the roots. I could not imagine why he had not fallen or how I managed to stay on. It would have been infuriating to fall off at the first fence in my first point-to-point and I was determined that Only Just should not make the same mistake today.

I need not have worried. Being so much smaller, he was easier to manage and after getting him well settled down as we approached the first fence, he cleared it beautifully.

The start of a Point-to-Point

Similarly with the second, after which we had to go up a hill, round some trees at the top, and then jump the open ditch. After this there was a long gallop downhill over ridge and furrow. Because of his short stride, Only Just made rather heavy weather of the ridge and furrow —altogether it was a bit of a scramble—but he jumped the fence at the bottom of the hill in good style, to make up some ground. At this time, we were tucked in nicely just behind the leaders. We completed the first circuit without any difficulty, although he did hit the second open ditch rather hard, and we began the second round over the same obstacles.

All went well until we came to the fence beyond the ridge and furrow again. Once more, Only Just's short stride unbalanced him and he struck the fence very hard, but he regained his balance and galloped on. Ahead of me I could see My Man going very well, looking as if he could jump yet a third circuit if he had to, and I was beginning to wonder if we should ever catch him up. Then all at once, as he negotiated a rather sharp turn before the last open ditch, his rider must have lost concentration momentarily, for she allowed him to turn a little too wide and we darted in on the inside. Although we drew level for a second, My Man jumped away from us again at the ditch.

There was only about a quarter of a mile to the finish now and we still had two made-up fences to jump. I knew that if we were to beat My Man this was the time to make our big effort. Fortunately, we had a long stride over both these fences, gaining about half a length at each. Edging closer and closer over the final stretch to the finishing post, we gradually drew level and then, as we reached the post, Only Just got his head in front—and we had won.

I do not think I had ever before felt so thrilled and surprised about anything. The owner, equally pleased with our success, hurried down to lead in the winner. All round us I could see people perplexed and puzzled, studying their programmes intently as they tried to find the name of this little horse, which had won the race at 12 to 1. And who on earth, one could imagine them thinking, is the jockey? I was so excited at being led into the winner's enclosure, that I could hardly unsaddle Only Just before being weighed-in.

A point-to-point programme will usually contain about five races, and there are a number of different types of races for the Hunt to choose from—Members and Subscribers; Hunt Farmers; Adjacent Hunts; Adjacent Hunts Farmers; Maiden Race, for horses which have not won a race before; Ladies' Race; Open Race for horses from any hunts, as opposed to those from adjacent hunts. There can only be one Open Race at each meeting and if, therefore, an Open Ladies' Race is on the card there cannot be an Open Men's Race, too. Some Hunts would rather have a Ladies' Race, because sometimes the owners of good horses prefer the lighter weights at which ladies are allowed to ride.

There is quite a lot of work involved with a point-to-point horse. I found this out from experience and I learnt a great deal from my mistakes. There are no short cuts to getting a horse really fit, and individual horses need different amounts of work and feeding. However, the final preparation is different from that which a horse receives for hunting or jumping. In the first place, to qualify for a point-to-point race a horse must have hunted ten times with one pack of hounds. If possible, it should be qualified by Christmas, or certainly by the end of the year, because it needs two months of concentrated preparation to get the horse in racing form before the point-to-point season begins in March. And there are one or two point-to-points even earlier.

The first thing I do is to get the horses up from grass in August and begin to harden them by road work, walking up and down the hills. Gradually they go on to more hard and concentrated food, as opposed to the grass and soft food they have been having during the summer. A point-to-point horse is usually a Thoroughbred and therefore often excitable, so it must have a quiet introduction to hounds. The cubbing season is ideal for this and it should go out as much as possible to get accustomed to the sight of hounds.

To get a horse really fit and well muscled up, it must be properly groomed during training and for at least one hour a day. I was very strict with myself over this when grooming Only Just and Dandy Dick and I used to set the kitchen alarm clock in the stable to make sure they got their full quota. Everyone who has groomed a horse for any length of time will know that it is an extremely good way of keeping the groom fit and healthy, too!

With the Hunt's opening meet, usually the first Saturday in November, it is vital to get the horse hunting and qualified as soon as possible, in case it should be laid up for any reason and so finish its qualifying spell too near to the opening of the point-to-point season. Moreover the weather is never very certain after the New Year and there is always the possibility of a freeze up. Ideally, it should have at least eight of its hunts before Christmas, if not all ten, with an interval of about a week between each, for if it hunts too often it may lose condition.

Assuming that the horse has qualified by Christmas, its amount of work may then be cut down to allow it to put on a little weight which might have been lost during hunting. Then comes the ordinary point-to-point training.

One of the secrets is to keep strict hours of work. Depending on how much work any one horse needs, it might last from one to three hours a day. One of the chief items on the training programme is plenty of walking to get the horse fit and hard, with an occasional long slow canter to build up muscle, and one or two short bursts each week to open its wind. Weekly bursts over hurdles or steeplechase fences are an important part of the training

The first jump in the Open Race at the Oxford University Bullingdon Club Point-to-Point at Crowell

for young horses since they must grow accustomed to jumping in a racing style rather than a hunting style. While out hunting, a horse will have been jumping carefully and high, but if it uses the same technique when steeplechasing it will waste time in the air. So the aim now is to get it to brush the tops of the fences and gallop on in its stride.

As the day for its first point-to-point approaches I give it half and full speed gallops to get its wind right, so that when the day comes it will be very nearly fully fit. Or maybe the final winding-up gallop might take place in another point-to-point, prior to the most important one which is the main objective.

Some horses can stand as much as a race every week, but this is very hard work for them because a point-to-point course is never less then three miles in length, and must include two open ditches. Since the course is usually over two circuits, the horses often have to jump both the open ditches twice. The course may be laid out over hills and include sharp turns. Then there are about twenty fences to jump with perhaps a water jump or a drop on the landing side of some of the fences. Jumping these obstacles, together with a long gallop of 3–3½ miles, is a severe strain on a horse.

When the race day comes at last, the horse has breakfast early and, if necessary, a short canter. This will depend entirely on the horse, but in any event should be done early enough to allow it to settle down again before setting off for the race. Normally it will be groomed and plaited up before leaving but, if the horse is anything like Only Just used to be, it might be as well to leave it as quietly as possible so that it will not realize it is going off to the races. The horse is then bandaged up, its blanket and head collar put on, and it is loaded into the horsebox.

On arrival at the point-to-point, the first thing to do is to visit the Stewards' Tent and declare your horse. This must be done about forty-five minutes before your race, otherwise the horse will not be allowed to run. To miss the race after months of preparation, apart from the anticipation, would be a terrible disappointment. So it is always wise to remember to declare a horse in good time.

You may have had a chance to walk the course the evening before but, if not, it is important to walk round on the day itself. In any case, there is no harm in having another look at it even if you have already been round, since the going might have changed over-night. Often a point-to-point has been lost because the jockey was uncertain about the exact position of the fences, the type of hazards he had to face, or the places to avoid to save time.

As the time for the race approaches, you should make sure that the horse is ready to walk round the paddock. Last minute delays and unnecessary hitches are upsetting for both horse and jockey alike, and can be so easily avoided with a little thought and care. When you have been weighed-in and passed, the horse is saddled up in the paddock and its number cloth put on.

It is often advisable to ride with a breast-plate on a race-horse to prevent the saddle slipping back. A race-horse, trained very fine, loses its fat and therefore has little flesh to keep the saddle in place.

Meantime the horses are being led round the paddock while the riders stand in the middle, tensed and waiting, trying to remember all they know about their rivals' mounts. 'That one jumps to the right, that one pulls to the left—if I'm behind him over a fence, I must try to be on the opposite side to the one he jumps to'—and so on. Then the owner of the horse you are riding is sure to have some last minute instructions.

The Mounting Bell rings, your horse is brought into the middle of the paddock, the rug is removed, girth tightened, and someone throws you up into the saddle. A moment's panic when you think it is going to buck you off in the middle of the paddock, but you quickly quieten it down and away you go for one more circuit around the paddock. The next thing you know, you are going down to the start, giving your horse a short canter to settle it down. Providing that you can pull up when you reach the start, you wait while the starter calls out the names and numbers of the runners. Then as he gives the order to line up, you concentrate on getting a good place, and keeping an eye on him: for as soon as everyone is in line, the starter signals, and you are off.

With a lot of runners it is essential to be quick off the mark and well away in a good stride. Otherwise your horse will be blinded by the rest of the field as it comes to the first fence. It may be excited and pulling hard, and you must use all your skill to get it on the job and settled down before that fence. Once over it, however, there is no need to push along in front just yet as long as it is galloping on in a nice easy stride. Unless the horse prefers to run in front, it is usually wiser to keep just in behind the leaders. Every horse likes to run differently and you should always take the advice of the owner who knows his horse's individual likes and dislikes.

Lengths can be gained by a bold and quick jumper that is ridden on at a fence. You will rarely ever come to harm if it stands back and jumps 'big', but it may fall if it puts in a short stride and hits the fence in front. By standing back, the front legs will normally reach over the obstacle, and therefore the horse will be unlikely to fall even if its hind legs do hit it. If you feel your horse is tiring, it may recover after being given an easy stretch over a few hundred yards to let it get its second wind. Never spare yourself or your horse if you feel it is full of running when you come to the last half mile or so. Help it all you can to gallop on, lack of will-power on the part of the jockey can lose a race. When you come to the last fence, ride at it as if it were not there. Having got round the rest of the course successfully, there is sometimes a tendency to play safe towards the finish and take a pull at the horse as you go to the last fence. This could be a fatal mistake, for not only may another horse jump past you as you slow up, but the caution might cause your horse to fall. Therefore, ride at the last obstacle with great determination and, although your horse will almost certainly be tired, you must always be ready to convince it that it can win the race.

After the finish, the first four horses are led up to the paddock and into the hurdles and the jockeys weigh in. Although for the purpose of judging the race, only the first three horses count, the fourth is always weighed-in in case there should be an objection to any of the first three. If not, however, the fourth jockey retires unobtrusively from the scene wishing, probably, that he had taken more trouble to walk round the course before the race, and had noticed that boggy patch which lost him valuable lengths.

In the meantime, your groom has taken the horse from the paddock and thrown a cooler over it. He will now be walking it round to cool off. A good rub down will follow and another walking spell to help its circulation, and to allow it to get its wind. It is very important to keep the horse warm and get it home as soon as possible.

When the horse is cool it should be given a drink of water with the chill taken off—just the same as after a tiring day's hunting—followed by a bran mash and then perhaps a hard feed later in the evening. Always make sure its ears are warm. If it breaks out, it must be rubbed down and dried off again. Before going to bed yourself, have a last look at your horse to make sure it is warm, dry, and completely calmed down.

Another way in which the preparation of a horse for racing differs from hunting is in its shoeing. A hunter has to wear thick, heavy, strong shoes to stand up to the mud and stones in the hunting field, and it may also have heels or calkins on the hind shoes and studs to prevent it slipping. Although a point-to-point horse can wear similar shoes when hunting, when it has qualified and is being prepared for racing it will have to wear much lighter ones. The light aluminium racing plates, however, will not be put on until the day before the race itself. These light shoes are necessary, because it is said that an ounce on the foot is equal to a pound on the back. If the horse is to have any road work after the race the racing plates must be removed first, and stronger shoes put back on again, because they will not stand up to a lot of hard wear. Continual changing of shoes should be avoided if possible, since it is inclined to weaken the thin wall of the horse's feet. When once our horses had been fitted with racing plates we tried to keep them on as long as possible, and were always careful to ride them only on grass with their light shoes after they had started competing in point-to-points.

After two or three races a horse might begin to lose condition. It may then need a rest for a while and, even if it does miss a race or two, it will be fitter to compete again towards the end of the season. The season is short and strenuous, and it takes it out of the horses to run in too many races. You will never find a steeplechaser running as many races as a point-to-point horse in such a comparatively short spell of time, and you have to do all you can to conserve your horse's energy and stamina.

When the racing season is over, the horse should be let down slowly. During the spring while it is racing, it is always a good idea to let it have five minutes' grass every day after working, since a few mouthfuls of spring grass keep it on its feed better than anything else, and also act as a natural tonic to the system.

At the end of the season, it should go gradually off its hard food on to soft food, until its diet consists of bran, hay, and grass. As its summer coat comes through it can be turned out on fine days.

I have often heard people say that point-to-point racing is a risky and dangerous pastime for amateur riders. Well, perhaps it is. But at the same time it is one of the most enjoyable sports I know, thrilling and exciting and, from the practical point of view, extremely good for one's riding. I have found that one is inclined to become over-cautious when show jumping, so a spell of galloping over fences, putting one's trust in God and the horse, does one a power of good. And aren't there dangers and risks in every walk of life, whatever one does?

Chapter Eleven

'RIDE 'EM COWBOY!' THE AMERICAN RODEOS

THE first rodeo show I saw in America was at Denver, Colorado. Denver is on a plain, and the massive Rocky Mountains rising up majestically behind it, together with the gay and colourful clothes worn by the cowboys and the crowds visiting this stock show, made a wonderful setting for one of the toughest riding sports in the world.

The rodeo has every ingredient to make it a real attraction. With its bareback riding, bucking broncos, bulldogging, calf roping, bucking Brahma bulls, and the characteristic pungent tang of peat and leather against a background of horses and cattle, together with the excited, cheering crowds, it has an atmosphere entirely its own. And to cap it all there is the breathtaking sight of the tough, lean, wiry cowboys astride these wild animals, performing prodigious feats of horsemanship.

Like many steeplechase jockeys, almost every cowboy seems to have broken most of his bones at some time or other, and nearly all of them walk with a limp. It is a sort of life that could be compared with that of a bull-fighter, who is past the peak of his career at thirty. Those of us who live more comfortably and less strenuously may wonder why these men take such great risks for so little return. Apart from the momentary success which they may achieve, I am sure they really love the life and find genuine friends and companionship amongst their fellow riders. As in show jumping, one may win a big event, but the next day or week, there is another event when one may not be so lucky. Their way of life is precarious in every sense of the word, but they seem to have developed their own philosophy to overcome the difficulties. If they win a big buck-jumping contest, the stakes are very high. If they draw a bad horse for their ride, or the judge does not like their performance, they get nothing. A fall might put them out of action for weeks. If they win, they are heroes until the next time someone else performs an even more sensational feat. These are the reasons, probably, that they are all so modest and diffident about their achievements, for they know that in their job the gap between success and failure is only a very narrow one.

The Denver rodeo is also a stock show and the judging and selling of the livestock brings farmers and dealers from all over America. There I saw the two tallest steers in the world, standing 19½ hands high, but although I was very interested in the agricultural side of the show, it was the signs saying 'That a-way (or this a-way) for the rodeo' that led me on.

Thanks to 'Western' films, we in this country are probably most familiar with the bronco-riding events. The term 'bronco' comes from the Spanish word meaning rough and rude, and that is certainly true of these wild, untameable horses. There are two classes, bareback and saddled, and in each case the cowboys draw numbers to see which horses they are to ride. This is where luck plays such a big part, because some of the broncos are known to be more difficult to ride than the others, so the riders have a fair idea in advance what their chances are likely to be.

The broncos are driven into chutes six at a time prior to the event. The high and narrow

Amateur rodeo with the working cowhands looking on at a friend successfully riding a bareback bronc

Saddle bronc riding at a Montana rodeo

wooden barricades keep them penned in so they cannot turn round. If it is a saddled event, the saddles are lowered on to the horses from above and another cowboy reaches through the barrier to tighten the cinch girth, and very often the horses start to buck furiously in the chute the moment they feel the constricting girth. The cowboy then climbs on to the top of the barrier, hitches up his chaps, pulls down his hat and sees that his saddle is well fixed before mounting his horse.

Each cowboy wears the same traditional dress—broad brimmed hat, shirt with a colourful knotted handkerchief around the neck, blue jeans, chaps—leather trousers that protect his legs—and high-heel boots. These high heels are very practicable, particularly in some of the other events when he has to dig them into the ground to get a grip.

As the cowboy lowers himself on to the back of the bronco, he takes a tight hold with one hand on the rope attached to the head collar. When he is sitting astride his horse, he signals to his pals that he is ready, and the chute door flies open. Out leaps the bronco, raising a cloud of dust, bucking wickedly, and using all the tricks it knows to throw the rider off its back. And for the cowboy it is not just a question of gripping tightly with his legs and hanging on. If he wants to win the contest there are certain rules that have to be obeyed.

First, the cowboy's free arm must swing backwards and forwards level with his shoulder throughout the ride, to show the judges that he is using only one hand to grip the rope, and that he is not holding the horse's mane. Second, with each buck he must rake the horse from shoulder to flank with his spurs, not to mark

This bareback bronc rider does not meet with the same success

it but to show that he is riding by balance and not by gripping with his legs. If he fails to do this, marks are deducted.

Sometimes the first buck as the bronco leaves the chute gets the cowboy slightly off balance, and then the bronco makes sure that he never has a chance to get back into the rhythm again. For rhythm of movement is the answer to staying on its back, and the cowboys who have the knack of it are the most successful. Even the best riders make mistakes sometimes or find themselves with a difficult horse. It is all in the luck of the game. Occasionally a horse comes out of the chute so fast that it falls over, and then the cowboy has to use all his ingenuity to fall clear and scramble away quickly before he is kicked by the flying hooves.

When the time limit is up, and the cowboy has succeeded in sticking to his bronco, there are two ways for him to dismount. If it is bucking beside the rails which encircle the arena, he can make a grab at the rope running round the top and let the horse buck away from beneath him. This is not always possible and there is always the danger that he will be kicked, so usually he tries to use the alternative method. For this, the two cowboy officials riding in the ring move up close alongside the bronco, and the rider takes one of them either round the waist or by the shoulders and jumps on to the back of his horse. He can then slide down the far side to safety, away from the kicking bronco.

One cowboy I saw bucked off his horse went straight up in the air like a rocket, turned a half circle, and came down with a terrifying crash on his head. We were all quite sure he must have broken his neck. However, after

A nasty moment for this cowboy as his saddle slips

being carried out of the ring like a corpse, he was back again within half an hour apparently none the worse for his mishap. If ever I needed convincing that these cowboys were tough, here was certainly proof enough, and even now I cannot really understand how he escaped so lightly.

One of the most difficult events is the bull-dogging in which the cowboy with his horse has to catch a steer and throw it. As the steer is released from the chute he gallops up beside it and, flinging himself from his horse on to the steer's back, clasps it round the horns and throws it to the ground. These steers are very heavy, much heavier, of course, than the cow-boys themselves, so skill and knack play a greater part than brute force. Here, as in the calf roping, the shortest time taken wins the event. It is judged from the moment the chute opens until the steer is thrown with its shoulder and flank touching the ground.

One of the events in which rider and horse have to work together in close co-operation is the calf-roping. First, the rider has to rope the calf from his horse using a lasso. Then he jumps from his horse and, taking the calf by the shoulder and flank, throws it to the ground. At the same time, the horse has to keep the rope, which is hooked over the horn of the saddle, taut and secure to allow the calf less liberty. To do this, the horse is trained to back away to take up any slack, while the cowboy runs down the rope to get hold of the calf. Throwing a strong bucking calf is no easy matter, and again it is skill and experience which count equally as much as strength. A good horse knowing its job will make the cowboy's task much easier. Once thrown, three of the calf's

Out of the chute like a charge of dynamite in an Australian rodeo

legs have to be tied securely together. To show that he has tied the legs properly, and not merely made a pretence of it to save time, the horse has then to walk up to the calf and, as the lasso slackens, the calf is let free. If it manages to struggle out of the short rope which is tying its legs, the cowboy gets no marks, or rather 'no time'.

Apart from the short rope, which he holds in his teeth, the rider starts with two ropes, one each side of the saddle, and if he fails to lasso the calf at the first attempt he can use his second rope. But, usually, if he misses with his first throw there is little point in trying again, for by then the calf is at the other end of the arena and too much time would be lost chasing after it. However, I did see one cowboy rope a calf with his second lasso before it had had time to think twice after it had dodged the noose of the first throw, but the speed with which he coiled and threw the second rope was unbelievable.

The most spectacular and dangerous display is the Brahma-bull riding, where the only security the cowboy has is a rope twisted around the middle of the bull. This rope is not knotted, so if the rider looses his grip for a second, the ends come apart and the rope drops off. He is only allowed to use one hand on the rope and the other arm must be kept swinging high above his head. Sitting on the uncomfortable back of a bucking bull must need extraordinary skill and nerve, particularly as many of them buck round and round in circles.

In the ring at the same time are two clowns who, although their antics make the crowd laugh, are there to divert the attention of the bull when the cowboy falls. To help them to do

Bareback Brahma bull riding

this, they have a small and strong barrel with no ends, in which one of them stands making faces at the charging bull. When the bull is a few inches away, the clown ducks down inside the barrel and as the bull's horns crash against it, it rolls over and goes tumbling around the ring with the clown wedged inside and the bull, very often, in close pursuit. Another favourite trick is for one of the clowns to climb inside the barrel while the other squats down on his hands and knees behind it, hiding from the bull. As he crouches there with his head on the ground, like an ostrich burying its head in the sand, the man inside the barrel moves it slowly to one side. The other clown is now completely exposed, with no protection whatsoever. At first he does not appear to understand his awful predicament, but as it gradually dawns on him he stretches out his arms and begins to feel for the barrel. Slowly he realizes what has happened—the barrel has gone and the bull is pawing the ground only a few yards away from him! Up comes his head, a look of mock fear transfixing his features, and with a cry of terror he rushes to the side of the arena and climbs up the fence.

All this buffoonery delights the crowd, but at the same time they know that it needs great courage and split-second timing if the clowns are to avoid a severe goring. The cowboys also know that their safety may depend on the clowns, even if they sometimes have to suffer from their practical jokes.

The most fascinating competition of all,

Calf-roping in Idaho. The horse is trained to keep the rope taut until the cowboy has thrown and tied the calf securely

however, is the one in which a cowboy has to cut out one calf from a bunch. In this, the patient training of the horses is seen at its best, for it is they who do all the work without any help from the riders.

The cowboy rides his horse quietly on a loose rein into the middle of a small herd of about nine yearlings. He selects his calf, indicates it to his horse, and from that moment it is entirely up to the horse to work the calf away from the herd to prevent it running back again. The cowboy plays no part in helping or guiding his horse when once he has shown which calf he wants cut out. If he makes any move to assist it, he loses marks. He has two or three minutes in which to show off the prowess of his horse, and in that time he is usually able to select about three calves. As each calf appears to be getting tired, he stops his horse, and the calf is allowed to return to the herd. Then he chooses another one.

Sometimes he might pick a bad calf which, once it is separated from the others, shows no inclination to return, and therefore offers no opportunity for the horse to display its technique. Immediately the cowboy leaves it and chooses a more lively one, but in so doing he must make it quite plain to the judges that he is allowing it to escape or else the horse will lose points.

The horses seem able to anticipate every movement of the calves and weaving swiftly in and out of the herd, they reminded me of graceful, light-footed ballet dancers, moving with smooth precision and faultless rhythm. Their dancing hooves and superb balance are a joy to see, and the unerring accuracy with which they manœuvre their calves away from the others, and the speed with which they dart first one way and then the other to prevent them returning, are not only a fine testimony to the men who have trained them, but a tribute to their own intelligence as well.

The rider of the winning horse in the cutting horse contest that I watched was a cowgirl, and I heard afterwards that she was riding with her leg broken in four places. Just before the finals of the event, her horse had slipped on the concrete outside the ring, and had fallen on her. She was helped back on to the horse and refused to see a doctor until after the competition. She must have been in agony, but no doubt her horse would not have performed so brilliantly with any other rider.

One of the most popular features of the rodeo is the competition for the young boys who belong to an organization not unlike our own Young Farmers' Club. A bunch of wild calves are let loose in the arena with the boys. If any of them can catch a calf and halter and hold it he is allowed to keep it. Then the following year he brings it to the rodeo to show in a special class. It is a very sound scheme since few of the boys could afford to buy their own calves, but it is a very difficult thing to achieve. Many of these boys are very small and they are in competition with heavy wild calves much stronger than they are. Even if they get near a calf, they have to throw it, in order to get the halter on it, and then the boy is lucky if he can hold on to the rope when the calf is on its feet again. Sometimes a frustrated 'capturer' is towed around the arena on the end of the halter rope, but if he can bring his 'prize' under control, he has a calf that may become the foundation of his future cattle.

The cowboys who compete at these rodeos have no management to look after them and are not paid a set wage. Each cowboy works as an individual, running his own affairs, deciding for himself where and when he will take part in a particular rodeo. These decisions must partly depend on the man's financial status at the time, because the entry fees for the various events are extremely high. On the other hand, the prizes are equally generous, but a run of bad luck, with no prize money coming in, could very quickly create financial problems. It must be difficult for a cowboy to make a start at all unless he is lucky enough to find someone willing to back him with an initial grant.

While walking round 'behind the scenes' at Denver, I was most impressed by the cowboys' energy. Every spare moment seemed to be devoted to polishing bits and bridles, so that they shone and glittered brilliantly in the sun. Western saddlery is in itself most attractive, with its hand-stitched leather and many varied trappings. This adorning a palomino or golden chestnut horse, mounted by a dashing cowboy in his gay and colourful dress, is something I shall never forget.

Another display I shall always remember was put on by a cowboy who, while convalescing after breaking his leg during a bucking-bronco ride, had trained his two sheep dogs to perform some extraordinary feats.

The display opened with the dogs skipping and doing balancing tricks, in themselves quite incredible, but the main event was yet to come. The 'curtain-raiser' over, we were asked to imagine that the cowboy and his dogs were spending a night out on the range. They came into the ring, and the cowboy got off his horse and began to unroll his blanket. In it he found two smaller ones which he gave to his dogs. Then he lay down and curled up inside his own blanket while the two dogs rolled up inside theirs. Then they all pretended to be fast asleep.

After a while, two men dressed as tramps crept stealthily on the scene. One of them drew a revolver, shot the cowboy, and made off with his horse. At once the two dogs sprang up, barking and growling angrily. One of them rushed after the second tramp, tore a piece out of his trousers, and chased him up the arena fence. The other dog ran across to the cowboy and started to give him 'artificial respiration' with his two front legs. In the meantime, the other one, having successfully disposed of his tramp, dashed after the horse, which by then had been abandoned, and, gripping the halter rope between his teeth, led it back to the cowboy. Now completely recovered after his dog's effective treatment, the cowboy got up, mounted his horse, and rode from the ring to the enthusiastic cheers of the crowd and the excited barking of his dogs, which, following closely at his heels, were thrilled with their brilliant performance.

All this, together with the Western Trail Riders in their luminous costumes, doing a square dance on their horses, and the grand parade with hundreds of horses and gaily dressed cowboys filling the whole arena, was only part of that great rodeo. Behind the scenes were the vendors of the enormous coloured spun sugar candies, hot dogs, and Coca Cola. Then the stands with all the western clothes on show. Leather frontier jackets with fringes on the shoulders and arms, so that the rain will drip off, without soaking through, hand painted bow ties, broad brimmed hats of every colour, cowboy boots with shaped heels and pointed toes, and shirts of a spectacular check or startling shade, with the practical stud fastenings instead of buttons.

When abroad, I have a weakness for collecting different tack for the horses. Among the stands, I found new nosebands, rawhide headcollars, various kinds of hackamores (bitless bridles), and plaited horsehair ropes and lassoes. As my dollars had run out before I had passed the counter with hand-made jewellery of Indian silver, my horses are not yet adorned with western saddlery. So, sadly, I had to wander away to look at the sheep and goats in another section of the show, for there I knew that I would not be tempted to acquire yet another souvenir from the Denver Rodeo.

Chapter Twelve

IMBER COURT

BY the entrance to the stables at Imber Court, the training centre of the Metropolitan Mounted Police, hangs the last of the old Bow Street Horse Patrol plates which, in those days, used to be displayed outside the lodgings of members of the Patrol. Today, well over a hundred years since the day that the Patrol became an integral part of the Metropolitan Force, this old plate is a reminder that, even though our way of life may have changed considerably, we still depend in part on the horse to maintain law and order.

It has been proved time and time again that when large crowds have to be controlled there is no substitute for the mounted policeman. The official estimate is that one policeman on horseback is worth ten to twelve on foot; unofficially the estimate is nearer twenty. We all have a very healthy respect for the size of a horse, and no one in his right senses offers any resistance when he feels its quarters brushing gently against him, urging him to keep his place in the crowd. That is the reason why the very presence of several mounted policemen is a deterrent to an angry mob. They command the respect of any crowd.

There have been some terrifying scenes when crowds have got out of hand. One of the worst times must have been at the first football Cup Final held at Wembley in 1923, when the vast crowd became completely out of control and swarmed on to the pitch, shouting and fighting and trampling each other down under foot. The next day almost every newspaper carried a photograph of this dense, black, frantic mass of bewildered football fans, and in the centre of the mob was a tiny white speck. It was just possible to identify it as a man on a horse—'The Man on the White Horse'—or 'Wellington of Wembley' as some newspapers christened him. It was this man—a mounted police officer—who played such a valuable part that day in clearing the pitch and restoring order.

The 'Man on the White Horse' was P.C. Scorey, Metropolitan Mounted Police, late Trumpet-Major, Royal Scots Greys. The white horse was Billy, winner of the King's Challenge Cup for Mounted Police at Richmond Royal Horse Show in 1928. To them, that Wembley Cup Final was probably all in the day's work, yet their achievements caught and held the imagination and gratitude of everyone who saw that extraordinary photograph in the newspapers the following day. Another picture hangs in the lecture room at Imber Court, not an 'action' one this time, but an ordinary photograph standing in its frame beside all the others. It shows P.C. Scorey mounted on Billy.

Mr. Scorey has been kind enough to describe for us what happened on that exciting afternoon:

'I was standing by at a local police station when word came through that the crowd at the Stadium had got out of control. Six of us were despatched at the gallop to reinforce the foot police. I managed to get Billy through the crowd which jammed the main entrance and, as we emerged inside the ground, an amazing sight met my eyes. The stands and terraces had overflowed on to the pitch—in fact, from where I sat on Billy, I couldn't see a single blade of grass! I worked my way through the milling mass of people until I reached the far goal-post. Then I started to push the crowd

P.C. Scorey on Billy trying to clear the pitch at the Cup Final at Wembley in 1923

slowly back towards the touch-line and told them to sit down. Gradually I began to get some order out of chaos. Billy could be temperamental at times but that afternoon he was good as gold. He pushed with his hind-quarters or leaned gently on the front row of people until they gave ground and I don't think he so much as trod on a single person's toes! He seemed to know exactly what was wanted of him and all I had to do was to sit there and let him do the job for me. Eventually the match got started, though I doubt whether more than one out of five people saw much of the game. I stayed down by the corner flag for the first half and Billy made a pretty good private grandstand! I shan't forget that afternoon in a hurry. It was a wonderful example of what a really well trained police horse can do in a critical situation. When Billy died in 1931, the Commissioner of Police presented me with one of his hooves mounted in silver. It is my proudest possession today.'

Imber Court came into being as a training establishment for the Metropolitan Mounted Police in 1921. Before that, the work of the Force was considerably handicapped by the lack of adequate facilities for riding and training, so the acquisition of this estate at East Molesey, in Surrey, was a vital necessity. Nevertheless, economy was obviously the keynote of the scheme. There are not many other stables in existence built entirely of concrete. The lay-out of the whole establishment has been compactly designed with an eye towards simplicity in working and easiness of access from one part of the building to another.

When I was shown round by Chief Superintendent S. T. Smith, who is in charge of the training establishment, I was at once impressed

The Musical Ride of the police horses

by the appearance of the stables. The arrangements for drainage, ventilation, and sanitation are excellent. The partitions of the stalls are higher than usual so that the horses cannot see each other. It has been found that they stand more quietly like this, and are generally much happier.

They eat and drink off the ground, out of concrete bowls built into the corners at the back wall. This is not everyone's notion of the ideal feeding method, but it does seem to have a number of advantages. For instance, the food cannot be thrown on to the floor and so wasted. A horse feeding with its head down is in the natural position for eating and digesting its food. However, there is the controversy that they are standing in a more balanced position when eating out of a high manger. The horses cannot injure their knees on these low mangers although they might put a foot in while feeding. Even then, there is little danger of injury as the edges of the bowls are bevelled and all angles are filled in with concrete.

I spent an interesting time in the indoor riding school watching the Riding Instructor, Inspector H. A. Griffin, and members of the training staff schooling their horses. These particular horses were near the end of their training period and had learnt much since the day they first arrived at Imber Court, probably from Yorkshire where a great many police horses are bred.

Two mottoes which the training staff might well adopt are 'efficiency with kindness' and 'training by reward', since these are the main characteristics in every stage of the horse's training. When the young horses arrive at Imber Court, they are raw recruits. They have to be turned into sensible and obedient mounts, just as able to stand like statues in the thick of

An instructor taking a class at Imber Court

London traffic, as they must be ready to manœuvre quickly in any direction to control an unruly crowd. The training must be done with kindness and patience to achieve these results.

Unusual circumstances call for unusual methods, and every possible device is used to train the horses to remain calm under all circumstances. They must learn to keep their heads when strange noises and disturbances are going on around them. Flag waving, rattles, fire bells, music, dummy crowds, flapping banners, and bunting—all these and other devices are used in their training.

First, however, the horses' confidence must be won before they can go on to this more specialized type of instruction. During the first stage of breaking in, the horses are driven in long-reins. In this way they are taught to understand and obey the voice and to grow accustomed to control from behind, by means of the long-rein. At this early stage, the horse does not have the weight of a rider on its back and is able to develop gradually and build up new muscles. Then the trainer begins to ride the young horse, making it supple and responsive and improving its balance.

The horse's intelligence develops as it learns to understand the aids for walk, trot, canter, and rein back. By means of poles and then tree trunks of varying thickness, put down at intervals, it learns to pick up its feet when walking over obstacles. It must be sure footed before starting work in London's busy streets. Also, by a progressive course of jumping, the back muscles are developed. When the trainers have their horses sufficiently obedient, they pass on to the specialized part of their training.

Gradually, the horses must learn to be calm

and collected in spite of the noise and confusion which goes on around them, in what has been picturesquely called 'the scare school'.

Flags and bunting are hung out around the riding school. Rattles and firebells compete with each other to make the most din. Men shout and cheer to give the effect of a crowd. Martial music blares out from an amplifier. In fact, the horses might well be actually taking part in a procession through the crowded streets of London—and an extremely lively procession it is too! Naturally at first they do not take very kindly to the clamour, but before long they learn to accept it as part of their everyday life, and come to look on the rowdy demonstrations with considerable disdain.

At the same time they undergo open-air training. They are ridden past dummies, and they must learn to walk up and push a dummy without showing any signs of fear or temper. Anything white in the road is liable to frighten a horse, so they are trained to walk past a tape on which a newspaper flutters backwards and forwards, like paper blowing about on the road. In time they take little notice of it.

They are taught many other lessons: such as passing by and through fire and smoke, standing still at level crossings, passing under a railway arch when a train is going overhead, walking through deep water, or standing still in it, walking up and down steps, climbing over steep banks and sliding down the other side, road work mounted and dismounted, and traffic sense out in the streets.

They spend their last month on advanced work. This consists of playing push-ball (to teach them to push hard when they are clearing a crowd), jumping, tent pegging, and sword and revolver exercises. At the end of it, they are ready to go anywhere and do anything with complete confidence and without the least show of fear.

The horses I saw Inspector Griffin and his men schooling indoors at Imber Court were nearly ready for their first job as police horses. At that stage they have about forty minutes in the riding school every day, where they walk, trot, canter, turn, and execute the left and right pass with a degree of instantaneous obedience that reflects great credit on their trainers.

After a breather, the gramophone was turned on and music echoed round the school from an amplifier beside us on the balcony. The horses took little notice of all the noise we were making. In fact, I am sure that one of them glanced up at us with a look of disdain as though he were saying, 'You can't scare me.'

Then out came the flags. With the horses now standing in a circle facing inwards, the Riding Instructor took two fairly small flags firmly in his hand and waved them in front of each horse's face. They did not actually turn away in disgust, but it was quite obvious that they were all far more interested in the tub of oats held by a groom standing behind Inspector Griffin.

The Riding Instructor then put down the flags and picked up a hand rattle, such as football fans carry. Standing a few yards in front of each horse in turn, he turned it slowly at first, gradually increasing the speed and noise, and walking towards the horse all the time. Eventually he held it a few inches from the horse's face without slackening its speed or the din it was making. But the horse was already looking eagerly over his shoulder at the tub of oats which was hovering a few feet away. You could almost imagine him saying: 'Oh, come on, you're not fooling anybody. Let's get on with it.' Then after a pat of encouragement from Inspector Griffin, the horse dived his head into the tub and helped himself to the oats. Obviously it was well worth the few seconds of slight discomfort.

Next, the fire-bell was brought out into the middle of the circle and one of the grooms grasped the rope and tugged on it furiously. At the same time the riders walked their horses in towards the clanging bell. Again there were no visible signs of reaction, except from one horse, which threw up his head and swung away. Immediately his rider turned him round to face the bell again, and he gave no more trouble. Then the tub of oats circulated again and all was well.

Chief Superintendent Smith showed us round the rest of the establishment, through the sick lines and into the lecture room, where instruction is given to the mounted policemen who go to Imber Court for an annual two weeks' refresher course. The far wall of this room is dominated by a skeleton of Royal, a horse that had spent his life in the Police Force. Royal is now used for practical demonstrations of anatomy and, therefore, he still continues to serve the Metropolitan Mounted Police.

Hanging on the wall above Royal is a 'mystery picture'. It is an oil painting of a horse's head found in the vaults of a church and presented to Imber Court by the vicar. No one has ever been able to identify the horse for sure, but from its trappings it might have belonged to one of the Welsh Regiments or probably to the Force itself.

One horse I saw with a famous name was Foxhunter, no relation to Colonel Llewellyn's champion show jumper, but named after him. Apparently, when Colonel Llewellyn saw Foxhunter at Imber Court he was struck by its likeness in many ways to its renowned namesake. Inspector Griffin told me the horse behaved well in traffic, but was rather naughty in crowds. This might have been caused by previous experiences in the hunting field.

Many of the police horses come from Yorkshire. Ideally they should be about 16 hands in height, with a good head, well-placed shoulder, short back, strong loin, and well ribbed-up middle piece deepening through the heart, muscular quarters and thighs, with a long forearm and a short cannon bone.

For dealing with crowded traffic in narrow streets a big horse is impracticable, so the smaller, compact horse is preferred since it can move quickly in and out of traffic. It must be quick off the mark, supple, intelligent, and imperturbable.

Many people think that all mounted policemen are ex-cavalry men. This is quite understandable when one sees how expertly they ride and control their horses. But, in fact, many of them have had no previous experience of horses or riding before they go to Imber Court. A few have been in the cavalry before, yet many ex-cavalry men do not qualify. For not only do the mounted police have to be the right height and physique for *general* service, but they must first undergo the ordinary police training. But no man, whether experienced or not, would have a chance of joining the Mounted Branch if he were not genuinely fond of horses.

Only the best type of men are selected. They must prove themselves good reliable horsemen, and their 'turn-out' must always be immaculate. They must take a real interest in their horses, and be considerate towards them. Sometimes you may see one of them standing dismounted in the road beside his horse, giving it a rest. Together with this understanding, it is the mounted policeman's tactful and effective control over crowds that wins the admiration of foreign visitors and British alike.

Often a true and lasting friendship develops between these men and their horses. There was one sergeant who, after riding his chestnut mare through the streets of London for many years, became a member of the permanent staff at Imber Court, and mare and rider were parted. A long time after, another mounted police officer went to Imber Court for training and took with him this same chestnut mare.

Anxious to see his old friend again, the sergeant went to the mare's box and spoke to her softly. At once she recognized his voice. She turned her head quickly, whinnying with delight, and nearly broke the rope that tied her, as she tried to turn to him. The sergeant put a lump of sugar between his lips, as he used to do in the old days and the mare at once took it from him, 'kissed' him affectionately, and in her own particular way showed him how very pleased she was to see him again.

So far as possible, when once a man has been given a horse, it is never taken away from him. In this way, each police officer can go through the whole of his service in the Mounted Branch with the same horse. They often become so attached to each other that there have been instances where the men on their retirement have pleaded to buy their horses.

The horses at Imber Court are all given names with the same initial letter according to the yearly batches in which they arrive. This year the letter is 'H' and three of the horses we saw being schooled were called Hawk, Holly, and Hilary. It is possible to gauge a horse's age roughly by this system, remembering that the letters I and X are not used owing to the difficulty of indexing them.

Almost all the 'departments' are concentrated under one roof. The Administrative Block consists of Chief Superintendent Smith's office on the right of the archway, beyond which are the stables, while on the left is the Administrative Sergeant's office and the pharmacy. Above these offices are flats for married members of the staff, and the single men are accommodated in a separate building not far away. The Chief Superintendent has his own flat on the top floor. There is ample space devoted to sports grounds and a fine pavilion overlooks the main ground on the left of the drive leading into Imber Court. This is where the Mounted Police hold their own show—The Imber Court Horse Show—each summer, attracting thousands of spectators from all over the country.

Although the buildings are of concrete, there is no lack of 'warmth' about this training establishment. With the grass lawns bordered by shrubs and flowers, which face the main building, and the creepers which climb over the face of the building itself, the impression is one of neatness and care. This emphasis on scrupulous tidiness might seem an unnecessary waste of valuable time to many people. But it is the pride in perfection that produces such a smart and efficient body of men to ride the London streets. Without this firm attention to every intricate detail, no matter how trivial it may seem to the onlooker and the uninitiated,

Policeman performing in a tent-pegging competition

the extremely high standard of which the mounted police have always been so rightly proud could never be maintained.

And as we drove towards the gates after our visit to Imber Court, even the stable cat, which had come out to watch us go, had obviously just been giving himself a thorough wash and brush-up.

There are over two hundred horses in the whole of the Metropolitan Force, spread out in units of three to twelve all over London. Recently, I was lucky enough to have the chance of visiting the Hyde Park unit, situated just by the Serpentine in ideal surroundings for the horses.

In this unit there are nine mounted police with their horses, and they work in shifts of three hours a day. When I went there, two were out escorting the Italian Ambassador to Buckingham Palace where he was to present his credentials to the Queen. We saw the coach driving through the park drawn by the bays, with a police horse trotting out in front to clear the way.

A few days before, these men had been involved in a demonstration at Westminster. One of the sergeants had lost his hat, and had his mackintosh torn, when some of the crowd tried to pull him off his horse.

Round the neck of each horse is a chain attached to the bridle and, although this adds to their smart appearance, it is really there for a strictly practical purpose. In a demonstration like the one at Westminster, some of the crowd may try to cut the reins and leave the riders with no control over their horses. When that happens, the chain acts as a spare rein. When necessary each police officer carries a large truncheon. The 'business end' is covered with soft soap, so that no one can catch hold of it and drag it from the officer's hand. They also have two small saddle bags in which are carried a waterproof saddle cover, a smaller truncheon, and a first-aid kit.

It was surprising to find how good the horses' legs were. In spite of so much road work and continual jarring on hard surfaces, their legs were quite clean and cool. Maybe it is because most of their work is done at the walk. They are shod with two mordax studs in each shoe to stop them slipping, with only very small studs in the front shoes. The stables were spotless and immaculately clean, with the straw neatly plaited at the back of each stall.

In the saddle room of the Hyde Park unit each man has his own locker. One officer had a cheque pinned on the back of the door of his, presented to him by grateful parents for rescuing their child from a runaway pony. He had galloped up alongside the pony in the middle of thick traffic and lifted the child off. Just before my visit to the Hyde Park police, they had been dealing with a case of neglectful use of riding-school horses. The horses were apparently in poor condition, not fed properly, sore and lame. It is just as well that the police can deal with these rare outrages, and they are to be congratulated on their immediate action in this case.

The unit for Central London is situated conveniently at Old Scotland Yard. This used to be Lord Lonsdale's coaching stables, one of the few left in London that have not lost their original intention. The horses are stabled up above the old coach house, now a garage and offices, and are led up a ramp covered by coconut matting to stop them slipping. The stables are divided in two parts with loose boxes on one side and roomy stalls for the greys on the other.

Many people argue that the horse has had its day, that it has outlived its usefulness except as a source of pleasure and amusement. They would get a true idea of the value of the horse if they could see the work done at Imber Court. Then the next time they saw a mounted policeman riding the streets, controlling the traffic, riding at the head of a procession, or subduing an angry crowd, they might try to imagine that he was no longer there and that twenty policemen on foot were standing in his place. Twenty men on foot to do the job of one man on a horse! And at a time when it is no secret that the police force is short of men.

London has shown that the horse still proves its value, even in this busy and mechanized age.

Chapter Thirteen

TEN THOUSAND MILES WITH TWO HORSES

THE extraordinary story of Professor A. F. Tschiffely's ten-thousand-mile ride on horseback from Buenos Aires to Washington fired the imagination of the whole world when it was published in book form as *Tschiffely's Ride* in 1933. This amazing journey was made with only two horses, Mancha and Gato, both Criollos, across prairie, mountain, swamp, and desert, in what was probably the last great equestrian feat the world will ever know.

To reach their destination, the travellers had to cross the Pampas, climb the Bolivian Andes, struggle through the sands of Peruvia, cross swinging bridges, swim crocodile-infested rivers, and, when once more in 'civilization', brave the dangers of fast-moving American traffic. Extreme heat, bitter cold, shortage of food, and lack of water did not deter them, any more than did blood-sucking vampire bats and the numerous species of unpleasant insects.

Tschiffely suffered from malaria, dysentery, and El Soroche, a type of mountain sickness, but the horses were never sick for one single day. They thrived equally well on the wiry grasses of the northern Pampas as they did on straw, rotten hay, fresh maize-stalks and the leaves of the palm-tree called Pindo. Changes of water did not worry them. Nothing worried them. No horse of any other breed could ever have endured the hardships which they accepted as a perfectly normal way of life.

To understand this journey, one must know something about the three travellers who undertook it. Aimé François Tschiffely came of an old Swiss family, but left for England before he was twenty to become an assistant master at a school in the New Forest. But he had been born with an adventurous spirit. His spells of schoolmastering were enlivened by such colourful interludes as signing on as a professional to a football club, and taking on all-comers at a boxing booth off the Edgware Road. Then he migrated to the Argentine. Good at games and fluent in several languages, he had no difficulty in continuing his career as a schoolmaster. The profession appealed to him particularly because of the long holidays, when he used to ride out alone into the prairies for weeks at a time.

Aimé Tschiffely

Mancha and Gato by the Cyclopean Ruins near Lake Titicaca

It was during these rides that the great idea came to him. He would prove to the world the unequalled and amazing stamina of the Argentine horse named *Criollo*. He would ride two of them alternately, one for his baggage, one for himself, all the way across the prairies, northwards twice over the Andes, among Indians who had never seen a white man before, down into the swamps and ravines dividing the two Americas, up through Mexico, and into the States.

His scheme was greeted with scorn and derision. It was 'impossible', 'absurd', he was obviously quite mad, yet at the end of it, two and a half years later, he was welcomed in America by the President and presented with the New York City Medal.

One might ask 'Why?' Why make the journey in the first place? What was the point of it, anyway? Surely there were better ways for a man as gifted as Tschiffely to employ his talents? Such questions remind me of the answer given by a famous mountaineer to the question 'Why do you want to climb Everest?' His reply was simple. 'Because it is there.' There was much of this same spirit in the character of Tschiffely.

The two ponies, Mancha and Gato were sixteen and eighteen years old when the ride began. To appreciate the reasons for the powers of resistance of the breed, it is necessary to know something about its origin.

The Argentine Criollos (Creole) are the descendants of a few horses brought to the Argentine in 1535 by Don Pedro Mendoza, the founder of the city of Buenos Aires. These animals were of the finest Spanish stock, the best in Europe at that time, with a large admixture of Arab and Barb blood in their veins.

When Buenos Aires was sacked by the Indians and its inhabitants massacred, the horses were left to wander over the country. They were hunted by the Indians and wild animals, they were forced to travel enormous distances in search of water, and the changeable climate killed off all but the strongest.

During the War of Emancipation and the various Indian wars, the Criollo horses carried out marches that would seem unbelievable if they were not now established facts. After approach marches covering hundreds of miles, they were still sufficiently fit and strong at the end to take part in vigorous charges against the enemy. At night they fed on whatever they could find. There was no massage nor grooming for them the next day, but hot, scorching gales, and burning, lashing sand storms.

Mancha and Gato had previously belonged to a Patagonian Indian Chief, and were then as wild as any horses could be. Even when Tschiffely first had them, they were far from tame although a long time had been spent on breaking them in. Mancha was red, with heavy irregular splashes of white, and had a white

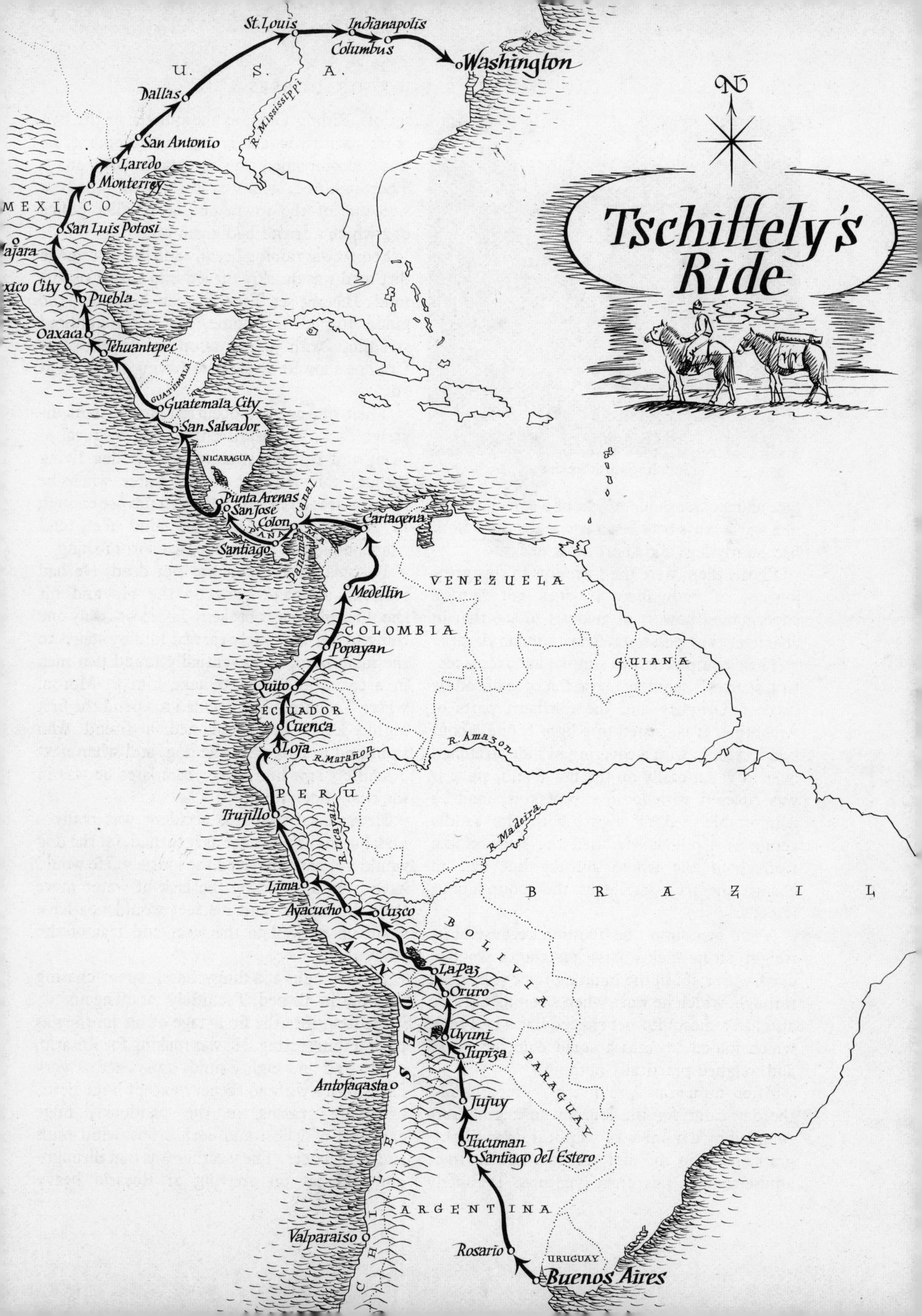

Tschiffely's Ride
N
St. Louis
Indianapolis
Columbus
Washington
U. S. A.
Dallas
R. Mississippi
San Antonio
Laredo
Monterrey
MEXICO
San Luis Potosi
ajara
xico City
Puebla
Oaxaca
Tehuantepec
GUATEMALA
Guatemala City
San Salvador
NICARAGUA
Punta Arenas
San Jose
Colon
Panama Canal
PANAMA
Santiago
Cartagena
Medellin
VENEZUELA
COLOMBIA
Popayan
GUIANA
Quito
ECUADOR
Cuenca
Loja
R. Marañon
R. Amazon
PERU
Trujillo
R. Ucayali
R. Madeira
Lima
Ayacucho
Cuzco
BRAZIL
BOLIVIA
La Paz
Oruro
Uyuni
Tupiza
PARAGUAY
ANDES
Antofagasta
Jujuy
Tucuman
Santiago del Estero
ARGENTINA
CHILE
Valparaiso
Rosario
URUGUAY
Buenos Aires

Saddling up Mancha

face and stockings. Gato was of a coffee colour, in a way a cross between a bay and a dun. Both had sturdy legs and short thick necks.

Those, then, were the travellers in this great journey of endurance. It does not require superhuman powers of analysis to see that in character they possessed many similar virtues.

Their equipment was simple, and, of necessity, sparse. Tschiffely chose the type of saddle used in Uruguay and the northern parts of Argentina. It consisted of a light frame, about two feet long, with a covering of hide stretched over it. It sat easily on the horse and, since it was covered with loose sheep-skins, made a comfortable bed at night, with the saddle acting as a pillow. He used the same saddle throughout the whole journey but had to change the pack-saddle in the mountainous regions.

A tent was out of the question because of its weight, so he took a large poncho, a woollen cloak with a slit in the middle to put your head through, which he wore when sleeping out. He also had a mosquito-net shaped like a bell tent, which folded up into a small compact space and weighed practically nothing.

After numerous preliminary preparations, the day came for the journey to begin. Surrounded by a number of sceptical Press photographers, who did not try to disguise their amusement at this crazy venture, Tschiffely set off. Riding Gato, as the quieter of the two horses, with Mancha acting as pack-horse, he was accompanied by a stable-boy on a Thoroughbred, who was to show him the best way out of the town, and a Belgian police dog which a friend had given him.

Soon it was raining heavily and the new-made dirt road was quickly turned into a river of soft mud. Having set Tschiffely on his route, the guide turned for home, his Thoroughbred steaming with perspiration while the two Criollos showed no signs of having travelled at all.

Their first mishap occurred almost immediately. Tschiffely heard a thud and a squeal of pain, and turning round, saw his dog flying through the air into a pool of water, where he lay as if dead. The dog had been unwise enough to get too near Mancha's hind feet, and Mancha did not encourage that sort of thing.

Fortunately the dog was not dead. He had received a severe blow on the hip and his shoulder blade was broken. There was only one thing to do. Tschiffely carried him by stages to the main road, and eventually found two men in a car who agreed to take him to Moron, where Tschiffely had decided to spend the first night. Later he telephoned a friend who promised to look after the dog, and when next Tschiffely saw him three years later he was in the best of condition.

He realized that this accident was really a blessing in disguise, for as it turned out the dog would not have survived the journey. He would have been affected by the lack of water more than the horses, and his feet would not have stood up so well to the wear and tear of the stony roads.

After a night at a dingy hotel, spent chasing the bugs in his bed, Tschiffely set off again.

He describes the first stage of his journey as most uninteresting. He was making for Rosario, a hundred and eighty miles away, across very flat country with no scenery except large herds of cattle grazing in the paddocks, huge expanses of wheat and corn crops, wind mills and wire fences. The weather was bad throughout, so that on arriving at Rosario heavy

Taking the two horses through the jungle

storms forced him to postpone the next stage for several days. At once the newspapers began to infer that he was getting 'cold feet' and would not get any farther. As it happened, he still had plenty of time to reach Bolivia in the dry season and there was no point in getting unnecessarily wet.

For over two hundred miles he travelled through fertile cattle and corn country, spending the nights at hospitable ranches or occasionally at one of the larger 'estancia' houses. Arriving at one of the latter on a Saturday night, he was lucky enough to see a camp 'fiesta' the following day, held to celebrate a good sale of cattle. The menu's special dish was 'carne con cuero', or roasted meat with the hide on, together with two or three lambs and a couple of sucking pigs as appetizers.

Later, when it became cooler, the horse racing began, consisting usually of contests between two horses over two to four hundred metres, with the jockeys riding bareback. He was interested to see that the betting on the last race was not nearly so brisk as on the previous ones, and on asking the reason was told that one of the horses belonged to the local chief of police, and was therefore unlikely to lose!

As they approached the desolate parts of Santiago del Estero, the land got more and more arid. He had taken the precaution of sending on ahead small bundles of hay to some of the stations of the railroad which crossed the region. The going was now atrocious. The horses raised thick clouds of fine dust, which at times were almost impossible to see through. The only inhabitants of this desolation were snakes, lizards, foxes, parrots and 'cuises', a kind of guinea pig. At one time he had to walk the horses through a swarm of locusts, which covered the ground like a thick grey carpet and clung to every cactus plant and shrub within sight. At first the horses refused to move, but when they realized there was no danger they went on through the mass of insects, crushing their bodies beneath their feet.

Soon the journey took them to the foothills of the Andes, through pine forests and deep gulleys or along rocky river beds. At times they were moving along narrow paths on mountain sides, with deep precipices falling sheer to the valleys below. It was often difficult to find the right trail and more than once they had to turn back. They had to ford many deep and dangerous rivers, and once the horse Tschiffely was riding lost his footing. The strong current carried them both down into a pool below the shallow rapids where they had tried to cross, but fortunately both of them struggled out of the water with nothing more serious than a thorough soaking and a severe fright.

By now the three travellers had become the best of friends. The horses had grown so fond of Tschiffely that he never had to tie them, and even if he slept in a lonely hut at night he turned them loose, knowing that they would be there to greet him the next morning.

The trail ahead would take them over great windswept mountains, as they made their way towards the Bolivian border, so their equipment had to be adapted accordingly. Although the packs had been quite adequate for travelling over the plains, a more suitable type of pack-saddle had to be substituted for the mountainous country. Additional firearms had to be bought. A cooking-pot, a kettle, and extra food was added to the kitchen equipment. At the same time, the weight of the pack had to be considered and kept down to the absolute minimum. The horse Tschiffely rode carried the money. Since in certain parts the Indians would accept only silver coins, it was extremely heavy. This horse also carried his documents (letters of credit, passport, maps, etc.), compass, barometer, and two or three books. To supplement the sheep-skins, he added a thick woollen blanket to his equipment. As protection against the rain, he bought a light rubber poncho. He also had a special mosquito net made to fit over his broad-rimmed hat and cover his face. Finally, to protect his face and eyes against the wind and sand, he bought a woollen mask and green goggles.

After attending to every minute detail, the horses were shod, then he packed up and saddled, and they set off on the perilous journey over the Andes down to the Pacific Ocean.

After travelling through the Humahuaca ('Weeping Head') Valley, they stopped for two days at some prehistoric ruins called Tilcara, and there Tschiffely had an accident that nearly cost him his life.

With a man to help him, he started to make a few excavations. As he put his hand into a grave they had just opened, a small thorn pricked one of his fingers and within a few hours a nasty infection set in, followed a few days later by blood poisoning. At first he ignored the swelling, but when the infection broke out in his other hand, in his face, and in his right leg, he realized it must be treated quickly.

There was no doctor anywhere near and he had to travel, a very sick man, for several days to a village where the local medicine man was quite unable to diagnose the nature of the poisoning. His treatment had no effect and he advised Tschiffely to return to Buenos Aires. But Tschiffely had no such intention. He had come so far and would go on whatever the cost.

They were now in high altitudes where mountain sickness affects strangers and all at once, while he was saddling the pack-horse, his nose began to bleed. He had 'puna', as they call it in that region. Sick and sad, he painfully wound his way up the rocky river-beds, until he suddenly came to the lonely hut of a mountaineer. There he was told about an Indian herb doctor of great fame in the neighbourhood, and agreed that someone should send for him. The doctor was an elderly and very poor Indian, of the most unprepossessing appearance. But Tschiffely soon found out that his appearance belied his ability, for, having diagnosed that the case was not a serious one, he put some steaming herbs over the open sores and within five days Tschiffely was able to continue his journey. The doctor asked one boliviano, roughly 1*s.* 6*d.*, for his services,

Drinking maté tea to the accompaniment of a guitar

including his eight days' 'travelling expenses' to and from the hut. When he received five times that amount, he was overcome with joy and gratitude.

After some extremely rough journeys and some very uncomfortable nights, Tschiffely reached the border village of La Quiaca, having successfully crossed the highest pass at a point called Tres Cruces (Three Crosses), over 11,000 feet above sea level. They had now covered about 1,300 miles.

Although he had been attacked constantly by mountain sickness and his nose had bled profusely, the horses did not appear to be in the least affected by the rarefied air. They had behaved quite normally even when crossing the high ridges and were, in fact, in better condition than when they left Buenos Aires. Nevertheless, Tschiffely was still doubtful whether they would be able to cross the main Andean ranges of Bolivia and Peru, which had to be negotiated before they came to the Pacific coast.

The next stage of the journey was marked by dangerous rivers, which had to be crossed, and giddy mountain sides, which had to be climbed. Once, all three of them had to lie huddled behind a rock near the summit of a high pass, while a hurricane blew and hailstones the size of small eggs rained down all around them. They passed through the country of the Aymará Indians, who were always having blood uprisings against their white oppressors. After a slight brush with the chief of an Indian settlement, Tschiffely fully expected to be attacked during the night, so, taking his rifle shotgun, and ammunition into one of the beehive-shaped ovens they used for baking bread, he set up a stronghold. But he was too tired to stay awake. The next morning he was woken up by an apologetic, shamefaced chief, who politely handed him boiled eggs, soup, and bread. The horses were standing nearby, calmly breakfasting off straw. Later, because of an Indian uprising, they went without food for forty-eight hours. At one point, Gato's instinct prevented them riding into a treacherous bog which lay beneath only four inches of water but which he refused to walk through. Despite the dangerous ground they had to cover, the horses were never bogged and by their instinct avoided the slimy pools beneath which lay the deadly quicksands.

And so they journeyed on, through the valley of Cuzco, the gateway to the ancient capital of the old Inca empire, and into the heart of the Andes. Here the trail was rough and varied. Sometimes they wound their way through narrow and deep valleys, with high rock walls on both sides, sometimes they were stumbling and scrambling up steep narrow tracks. Dripping with sweat, they had to stop frequently to recover their breath. Often the track was cut out of a perpendicular mountain wall, with a steep fall down to a river. In some places the trails were so narrow that the pack animal had to walk near the edge to avoid bumping against the rocky wall. It would have been impossible to pass any other animals coming in the opposite direction.

At one point, Gato stepped too near the edge, lost his footing, and, sliding over the side, rolled down towards the edge of a deep precipice. If a solitary sturdy tree had not stopped his fall, he would most certainly have been killed.

Vampire bats were now causing them a lot of trouble, and often in the morning Tschiffely found the horses clotted with blood that had oozed out of the small circular holes the bats had bitten into their backs and necks. At first, he was puzzled that a horse should allow such a big animal to bite it, when it defended itself against an insect or a fly.

These bats usually live in deep valleys where, owing to the hot, damp atmosphere, the horse perspires even at night. They have a way of flying around the horse until he becomes drowsy, and, as they hover near the spot where they intend to bite, they gently fan the air against their victim. As soon as the horse is bemused by the pleasant, cool sensation, the vampire settles down gently on him and bites through the hide with its sharp teeth, all the while keeping up the fanning with its wings.

The bats attack not only horses and cattle, but also poultry. The natives say that a vampire will always return to the same wound for its next feed, and so they smear a mixture containing strychnine over the bite. When the bat again attacks, it is poisoned.

Tschiffely eventually found that the best way to keep the pests from his horses was to rub them thoroughly with well-crushed garlic, sometimes adding a sprinkling of Indian pepper. It was useless to cover the horses with rugs for, owing to the heat, they only shook them off again. Strong smelling disinfectant acted as a deterrent, but was apt to burn the horses' skin.

They were bitten several times just at the point where the saddles pressed, and it was difficult to saddle them without giving them a sore back.

After a brief stay at Lima, where he saw his first bull-fight, Tschiffely set off across the sandy deserts of the Peruvian coast. Reaching Paramonga, he found the fortress in the throes of bubonic plague and was immediately faced by a difficult decision. The next stage of the journey was to take him north across a vast desert, with a hundred miles from one river to the next. Since there would be no water on the route, he had decided to make the long ride in one journey, and to do this with any degree of safety it was necessary to wait for the full moon. But the moon would not be at its highest for four days. So for four whole days and nights he had to stay in the plague-ridden fortress, taking every possible precaution, yet never certain that he would not be the next victim. And to increase his doubts and fears, he was told that the sandy wilderness he was about to cross was called 'Matacabello'—Horse-Killer.

Crossing a bridge in Peru where even a tightrope walker might not always be at ease. This wobbly structure sways so much that nervous travellers are often blindfolded, strapped to a stretcher, and carried across by Indians

But at last he was ready to start. Since he was not carrying water for the horses, he gave them nothing to drink the day before so that they would take a good long drink just before setting off. For himself, he took two bottles of lemon juice in the saddle-bags and a few pieces of chocolate that had been in his pack for some days. As the sun began to set, they crossed the river and walked slowly into the rolling desert, an interminable, limitless carpet of sand stretching forward as far as the eye could see, to where the next river lay, a hundred miles away.

Soon they were twisting and snaking through high sand dunes, taking advantage of the wet sand on the beach for a canter whenever possible. Often they came to rocky places or to land-points which stretched far out, and had to make detours inland over considerable distances. When the moon went down shortly before dawn, they halted for a while in the darkness.

The first rays of the morning sun were hot and the day turned out to be a real 'scorcher'. As if sensing that this was a test for them, the horses plodded on gamely until about one hour after noon, when they suddenly lifted their heads and sniffed the air. At once they began to hurry forward and tried to break into a gallop. An hour later Tschiffely knew the reason for their sudden eagerness. With the instincts of the wild horse, they had scented water long before he could see it, for there in front of them was the river. It had taken them twenty hours to reach it.

After a long drink, the horses were turned loose in a small field with good grass, and when they had rolled, stretched, and shaken themselves they started to eat. They were obviously no more upset by their long, arduous trek than if they had just returned from a short canter.

Physically and mentally exhausted by the strenuous ride, Tschiffely sat down on his saddles to rest while a woman in a hut cooked him some food. When he suddenly woke up hours later, it was evening. The woman had kept the food warm for him, and after the first mouthful he did not stop eating until the last grain of rice had disappeared.

After a near-drowning in a deep, fast flowing river, they came to Trujillo, one of the biggest towns in Peru and about half-way between Lima and the border of Ecuador. There Tschiffely rested for a few days, before once more setting out across the hot sandy wastes and into the fertile Chicama valley.

For a while now he was able to enjoy decent sleeping facilities, good food, and an occasional bottle of cold imported beer. The fact that he was once or twice under suspicion as a Chilian spy was nothing compared to the dangers he had just left behind him.

He was now faced by his most formidable water obstacle, the river Santa, a wide, swift river in full flood, a roaring, seething, tumbling mass of treacherous water, with jagged rocks lying just below the surface waiting to rip a horse to pieces if he swam over them, and large whirlpools where two currents met.

In normal times, the cattle were swum across by 'chimbadores' who earned their living in that way, but when the waters were high nobody ever dreamt of trying it. The best of these men was consulted. After studying the river carefully, he said it was unlikely that any animal could reach the other side. But Tschiffely had confidence in his horses and decided to make the crossing the following morning.

The news spread like wild fire, and when he arrived at the river bank there was already a big crowd there to see the show. Some had come on mules or horses, some on foot. Even the far bank was crowded with spectators, who had arrived in plenty of time to make sure of getting a good place for the dangerous crossing. Tschiffely unsaddled and the kit was sent across by the normal route, a basket attached to a high cable. Just as he was getting ready to cross himself with the horses, a local official came up and told him bluntly that he would not allow him to enter the river. The whole idea, he said, was rank suicide for one who did not know the tricks and dangers of the wild waters.

Dumbfounded by this sudden change of heart, for previously this man had been most friendly towards him, Tschiffely had almost resigned himself to the thought of waiting for several weeks until the river went down, when he noticed a 'chimbador' standing near. He went over and offered him a large sum of money if he would swim the horses across. After much persuasion he eventually agreed and began to make his preparations.

These included a long searching study of the river, and the despatching of look-outs up-stream to give warning of any stray branches or trees that might come suddenly floating down. Ready at last, Mancha was coaxed into the water, the man mounted and, with Gato following loose behind, the journey across the roaring torrent began.

The people on the bank were making bets as to whether the horses would get across, as Tschiffely stood anxiously watching the little party cautiously picking its way through the seething water. Like hours, the minutes slowly ticked away until with a loud cheer from all the spectators, both animals waded out on the other side nearly half a mile downstream. The Rio Santa had been conquered in full flood. Tschiffely crossed by the cable, collected Mancha and Gato, who seemed none the worse for their unpleasant experience, and went on his way.

After many long journeys through sandy deserts, across more wide rivers and through thunderstorms in the hot, humid climate of the tropics, they crossed the equator at Quito, 4,500 miles from their starting point.

The next stage took them over the border into Colombia, across the hot Patia valley into broken and mountainous country, until at last Tschiffely was able to begin thinking about making his plans for the crossing to Panama. He found that owing to vast swamps and virgin forests, a land crossing was out of the question, so reluctantly he decided to carry on as far north as possible and then take ship across to Colon. But before reaching Cartagena, from which the crossing was to begin, the travellers had first to sail some way in an ancient barge up a crocodile-infested Magdalena river, under the most primitive conditions with scarcely any protection from the hot sun for either Tschiffely or his horses. However, after another overland journey, Cartagena was safely reached, and they went aboard the Royal Netherlands ship, *Crynsson.*

During the journey, Tschiffely thought back on the many incidents and adventures they had experienced during the 5,500 miles trek from one end of the South American continent to the other. The whole thing seemed like a dream, sometimes pleasant, but more often like a nightmare.

They docked at Colon and Mancha immediately took a strong dislike to being hoisted off the ship. The moment he was lowered on to the concrete dock, he bucked madly right through the customs house, scattering passengers and officials in all directions, and, undaunted, continued his war-dance among the sprawling luggage and trunks. He calmed down when Tschiffely caught him, but it took quite a lot of petting to make him understand that those sort of tactics were not generally considered the best for making friends in a foreign country.

At the end of November, when they arrived at Colon, the rainy season was at its height, so they had to wait some time for the dry season before attempting the crossing to Costa Rica. The horses were happy and enjoying themselves, so Tschiffely had a chance to do the same. But after frightening the wits out of some well-dressed American women by his rough appearance, he decided that first of all he had better buy some new clothes and have a haircut.

The time came to move on, and he followed a good road which ran into the interior of Panama as far as Santiago. Unfortunately, it was difficult to find fodder in many parts, and to add to the difficulties the horses were sometimes literally covered from head to tail with wood-ticks, and other equally unpleasant insects. This problem was solved by using a mixture of petroleum jelly, sulphur, and camphor, lightly applied to their coats. He sponged himself every night with creosote diluted with water. Nevertheless, he was often full of little red ticks himself, which fastened on to him in the grass shrubbery where the horses grazed. Round his waist, where his belt rubbed and pressed, he was raw and bleeding. The perspiration running into the sores burnt so much that he had to apply distilled water with a six per cent solution of cocaine to get temporary relief.

After riding through jungle-land for two days they came into open prairie, passing through primitive villages, and finally reaching Santiago. Here the road from the Canal Zone came to an end and the country changed to hills, shrubbery, and trees. From Santiago they followed a narrow trail through shady tropical forests, with enormous creepers twisting up round the trees, and crossed several deep rivers.

It was here that Gato suffered when the bottle of creosote broke in the saddle bag and poured down over his left flank. By the time they reached a stream and Tschiffely was able to wash it, a huge swelling had come up, and after a few days an enormous piece of hide peeled off, leaving Gato with a very nasty raw patch. It was some time before it healed and several months before the hair had fully grown again.

The massive roots made progress through the forests slow and dangerous. Both horses caught their legs in them frequently and each ripped off a shoe. Tschiffely had no spare sets with him, so he was very relieved to reach David, in the interior of Panama, where an American Army official had sent four sets on ahead.

Realizing that the next lap of the journey through the jungles and over the continental divide would be difficult and risky, he engaged a guide, a half-caste Indian about fifty years old. He had to buy a sturdy pony for him, because his pack was too much for the already heavily laden horses. Like most jungle men the

Indian did not often ride it himself, usually preferring to go on foot leading the pony with one hand and holding his 'machete' in the other.

They began the journey through the forests, along narrow trails that led in all directions. Food was very scarce and soon there was nothing left in the saddlebags but clothes, instruments, and ammunition. The farther they went, the denser became the jungles and forests. They twisted continually through thick vegetation with the roof formed by the high trees above them obliterating the light and the sun. They shot wild turkeys for the cooking pot. Once when they were nearing a little stream the horses suddenly became very nervous and troublesome. Mancha had been on edge for some time, and when they came to the muddy edge of the stream the guide pointed to some spoors that were still filling with water, and said 'tigre'.

With their supplies running low they went out hunting wild turkeys and pigs. There were none to be found so they shot some monkeys and ate them instead. Coming to a small, clear river they undressed before crossing it. Tschiffely saw an inviting pool a few yards upstream and decided to have a swim. Just as he was about to dive in, the guide shouted 'lagartos!' (crocodiles). He looked into the pool and saw two or three dark shapes lurking just below the surface. He fired at the biggest with his revolver, and in a second what had once been a calm, still pool became a seething, bubbling flood, with the wounded crocodile lashing about madly until he finally dived down out of sight to the bottom.

Tschiffely was now beginning to worry that they would not reach civilization before the rainy season set in again. The country was very hilly and the horses frequently stumbled and fell, and because they had to move cautiously their progress was naturally slow. His boots were falling to pieces and some of the saddle-straps had rotted and broken. They were now making for San José, the capital of Costa Rica, but to reach it they had to cross the high and difficult 'Cerro de la Muerte' (Death Mountain).

Before they reached the foothills, it began to rain and the horses could hardly stay on their feet. After scrambling a few yards, they all had to stop for breath and steps had to be hacked to let the animals get a grip with their hooves. They went on like this for hours, until at last they reached the higher altitudes and entered the oak forests. Although the temperature was now cool, the perspiration was pouring off them. The guide's pony had fallen so often and was so tired that it began to refuse to get up. Every-time it fell, one of the men had to pull at it in front while the other helped the animal to its feet by lifting its tail. Late in the evening they came to a shelter built by Government men some years before. All they could find for fodder were small palm leaves, but despite their toughness and bitter taste they had all been eagerly devoured by morning. The men built a fire and cooked a hen for their supper.

After another difficult day, they found shelter again the following night. It was bitterly cold and a little spring nearby was completely surrounded by ice. The horses were used to this, and they pawed and broke the ice. The guide's pony, on the other hand, could make nothing of it and would only drink out of Tschiffely's sombrero. Later the horses were turned loose on some coarse grass growing nearby. They were now over 11,500 feet above sea level at a point known as 'Muerte' (Death).

The next day they began the descent, slipping over rocks and stones and picking their way gingerly step by step over the rocky crags. Suddenly a terrific downpour set in, with a strong wind that made it impossible to protect themselves from the icy water which was quickly soaking through to the skin. It was a miracle they ever got the horses safely down the slopes.

By evening, Tschiffely's boots were in shreds and his feet had been cut to pieces by the sharp rocks. The rain lasted all night and he realized that they had just beaten the rainy season—by twenty-four hours.

Before setting out the next morning, he had to grease his sore feet with the fat from their last chicken, and patch up his boots as best he could. The going was atrocious and in many places they waded up to their knees in mud. At last they came to the first habitations, two lonely huts, and from then on the trail improved until they reached the first outpost of civilization, a village consisting of a few houses.

Not far from there they met a party of men hunting a tiger. It had apparently killed several cows and they were after it with rifles and shotguns. As Tschiffely and his guide moved on down the trail, they saw the tracks made by the tiger clearly imprinted in the soft mud.

As soon as they reached the first big village, Tschiffely telegraphed the Argentine minister in San José to let him know they had arrived safely in civilization. Meanwhile, the local policeman had put his hut at their disposal and they were able to clean and dry their drenched and mud-soaked clothes. The policeman then prepared them a meal and fed the horses.

In spite of the torrential rains, they covered the remaining eighty miles to San José in two days. Towards evening on the second day, they looked down from a mountain top on to the town stretched out in the vast valley below, and as the sun broke through the clouds and the wonderful view was unfolded before their eyes, they began the final descent.

After a few leisurely days in San José, enjoying the 'social life' of the town in the city clothes he had sent on from Panama, Tschiffely prepared to move on through Nicaragua. But everyone advised him against the trip. A revolution was taking place in the very parts he wanted to ride through! But he was determined. It was, after all, a very short trip through Nicaragua. He would not let a little episode like a revolution upset his plans.

It was not until the revolutionary and government representatives in the town put it to him in the strongest possible terms, coupled with a wire from Buenos Aires advising him not to take the risk, that he admitted defeat and agreed to travel the next stage by ship.

Through the republic of San Salvador and across the border into Guatemala City, the trail led him without serious mishap. Some way into the Guatemalan territory he was stopped by a group of soldiers, whose leader demanded to see his authority for carrying fire-arms. But he had no special licence, so as a substitute he took an old hotel bill from his pocket and showed it to the man. That was sufficient. The imposing-looking document did the trick and he was allowed to continue. Once again his instinct had not failed him. None of the soldiers could read.

From the first moment they stepped on Mexican soil at the bridge near Tuxla Chico, until they crossed the international bridge over the Rio Grande into Texas at Laredo, Tschiffely says the Mexican hospitality almost embarrassed him. Wine, food, and cigars appeared as if by magic at the least excuse, and he must have been embraced a hundred times in true Mexican style, with everyone giving long and prolonged 'vivas' for the Argentine republic. Army officers and officials gathered to welcome him to their country, and when Gato went lame with an abscess near the quick of the hoof, a vet from the Mexican army went along immediately and treated it. But just as the invalid was recovering, a more serious accident happened to him. The horses were stabled under a shed in the back-yard of the dirty hotel where Tschiffely was staying at the time. Going into the stable to feed him one morning, he found to his amazement that a mule was tied next to Gato and that he was cut and bruised where he had been kicked during the night. The mule's spiked shoes had cut deep into his flank and there was a nasty cut in the left knee. The pain had made him put all his weight on to the right side where the previous trouble had been.

Gato's knee became so bad that he was unable to lie down, and soon a terrible abscess set in. For a whole month, Tschiffely worked on him, but he looked so bad that everyone who saw him thought the kindest thing would be to put him out of his misery. Tschiffely would not, of course, hear of this. He realized that the horse's recovery in the bad climate was impossible, so he got in touch with the Argentine Embassy in Mexico City and arranged to send the cripple by train. Luckily, they had reached Tapachula, where the line from Guatemala passed, for if the accident had happened anywhere else he would have had to sacrifice the horse.

The question now was whether two of them could get through on their own as far as Mexico City, after which the rest of the journey would be comparatively easy. Would the swamps along the coast and the mighty Sierra Madre rob them of the victory that was now almost in sight? Although the month's delay had caused him to miss the best time for travelling along the swampy coast, and the rainy season had set in, he was determined to continue. After all the adventures that lay behind him along the vast stretches of country he had already successfully travelled, he was determined that, come what may, he was not going to be beaten now.

The next part of the journey was a difficult stretch, but Mancha plodded on gamely through the thick mud. The rain increased daily. At times the almost unrecognizable trail wound through jungle forest, where it was impossible to ride. Branches, twigs, and leaves obstructed their path and the guide had to use his machete to clear a way. Often they had to wade through slime and water up to their waists.

They travelled in these conditions until they reached a place called Tonala, where everyone turned out to greet them and to admire Mancha who, possibly because of his colour, was immediately christened 'El Tigre de las Pampas'. Tschiffely was warned that, with the outbreak of the revolution, bandits had become very active in the neighbourhood, and, stopping farther on at a place called Jalisco, the general in charge of the troops there told him that if he went any farther he would most certainly be attacked. Late one evening the general called on him to say he had received orders from the War Department to supply him with an escort. From there to Oaxaca, up in the mountains, he was escorted all the way. He was quite certain that if it had not been for these soldiers, his horses would undoubtedly have been lost to the bandits.

From Mexico City, where a banquet was given in his honour, Gato, in the best of spirits, joined them to cross the Rio Grande into Texas and victory was really in sight at last. Welcomed with lavish hospitality wherever he went, he began to wonder if he ever would reach his goal! And before he reached it he had one more unpleasant incident.

He had already had considerable trouble with 'road-hogs' driving at a furious pace along the roads he was following, some of them deliberately pulling across the road to 'shave' his horses. One of them went one further. His car hit Mancha violently, knocking him down and making a gash in his flank. The driver did not stop, but before disappearing round the bend he honked his horn and waved his hand at them. No doubt he thought the whole thing a huge joke. Fortunately, Mancha recovered after the initial shock and, although he bled profusely, no bones were broken.

The night before he arrived in Washington, a newspaper man motored out to interview Tschiffely, and carefully explained the road he should follow the next day, so that he would not miss all the people who were coming to meet him. But he did go the wrong way, and eventually had to telephone the Argentine Embassy to ask for a rescue party to come out and find him.

In Washington he was interviewed, photographed, taken here, taken there, and for several days was completely enmeshed in the social whirligig. He went on to New York where he was presented with the New York City Medal. Returning to Washington, he was received by the President at the White House and later delivered the opening lecture to the National Geographic Society.

And Mancha? How was he enjoying himself all this time? Very much it seemed, for when Tschiffely went to visit him on Governor's Island, where he was stabled with the army, a sergeant greeted him with—'Good morning, sir, would you mind telling me what kind of a hell-pet your horse is supposed to be?' He went on to explain that, thinking Mancha should have a little exercise, he had tried to ride him. At this the horse had 'gone off like a stick of dynamite'. After three unsuccessful attempts, the sergeant had given it up as a bad job. He was somewhat consoled, however, when Tschiffely explained that he was by no means the first to be treated in this way—it was just Mancha's disrespectful attitude to strangers.

Gato rejoined them after travelling from St. Louis by rail, a pack horse being an unnecessary risk on the busy highways. So all that remained was the journey back home to Buenos Aires, this time in the comfort of the liner *Pan American*. A large crowd was waiting for them when they arrived, and as Tschiffely walked down the gangway he was swept off his feet and trampled on. Only slightly hurt, he was quickly rescued and was the first to see the funny side of it. After the extreme hardships and dangers he had endured, it was certainly a rather ironic home-coming!

It was suggested to Tschiffely that the two horses should be put in a public park where people could go and see them, but he decided it would be kinder to return them to the pampas where they could enjoy the life which was natural to them. So they went south to a beautiful 'estancia', where they were to spend the rest of their lives in peace and comfort.

Late one evening, in the red light of the sinking sun, he went to see Mancha and Gato for the last time. They seemed to sense his sadness at the coming parting, for they rubbed their noses against him and nickered softly in his ears.

Then, at last, as the sun began to slip slowly down behind the vast expanse of the pampas, he jumped on to his horse and, with a last wave of his sombrero and a final word to his two faithful friends, Tschiffely rode off towards the setting sun.

THE END